Offering of shell and jade consecrated a sacred structure in Copan, Honduras.
FOLLOWING PAGES: Sunset ignites ruins of Uxmal in Mexico's Yucatan state.

LOST KINGDOMS OF THE MAYA

by Gene S. Stuart and George E. Stuart

Prepared by the Book Division
of the National Geographic Society
Washington, D.C.

LOST KINGDOMS OF THE MAYA
By Gene S. Stuart and George E. Stuart

Published by
The National Geographic Society
Gilbert M. Grosvenor, *President and
Chairman of the Board*
Michela A. English, *Senior Vice President*

Prepared by the Book Division
William R. Gray,
 Vice President and Director
Margery G. Dunn, Charles Kogod,
 Assistant Directors

Staff for this book
Ron Fisher, *Editor*
John G. Agnone,
 Illustrations Editor
Jody Bolt, *Art Director*
Victoria Cooper, Bonnie S. Lawrence,
 Researchers
Edward Lanouette, Bonnie S. Lawrence,
 Gene S. Stuart, Jennifer C. Urquhart,
 Picture Legend Writers
Carl Mehler, *Map Research*

Sandra F. Lotterman, *Editorial Assistant*
Karen Dufort Sligh, *Illustrations Assistant*
Lewis R. Bassford,
 Production Project Manager
Heather Guwang, H. Robert Morrison,
 Richard S. Wain, *Production*
Karen F. Edwards, Elizabeth G. Jevons,
 Artemis S. Lampathakis,
 Teresita Cóquia Sison,
 Marilyn J. Williams, *Staff Assistants*

Manufacturing and Quality Management
George V. White, *Director*
John T. Dunn, *Associate Director*
Vincent P. Ryan, *Manager,*
 and R. Gary Colbert

Jolene M. Blozis, *Indexer*

*Still wearing a blanket of soil,
Maya gods and rulers appear
on a stucco facade perhaps 1,500
years old, found in 1990
in Campeche state, Mexico.*

HARDCOVER STAMP: A BALL COURT MARKER FROM COPAN;
ADAPTED FROM A DRAWING BY BARBARA FASH

KENNETH GARRETT (ABOVE AND PAGE 1); DAVID ALLEN HARVEY (PRECEDING PAGES)

Color spills from the hands of traditional Guatemalan weavers as they hold aloft a loom.

Curving past the ancient ruins of Yaxchilan in Mexico, the Usumacinta River flows through western Maya lowlands. Explorers and artists in the 19th century helped bring Maya ruins to light; 20th-century scholars in many fields illuminate the culture. A stone head from Copan (opposite), reflected in a mirror in the British Museum, may portray a ruler of the city. *FOLLOWING PAGES: Sweat and toil have supported Maya society for nearly 4,000 years. A farmer in Solola, Guatemala, near Lake Atitlan, tills a field of rich volcanic soil.*

INTRODUCTION

by George E. Stuart

March 1, 1517, somewhere off the northeast coast of the Yucatan Peninsula. Three small wooden ships under the command of Francisco Hernández de Córdoba rock gently in the turquoise waters close by a shore unknown to them before that day. On board one vessel, soldier and future historian Bernal Díaz del Castillo squints toward a shimmering skyline that rises above the trees beyond the beach. "As we had never seen such a large town in the island of Cuba nor in Hispaniola," he later recalled, "we named it the Great Cairo."

Córdoba's men never had the chance to inspect Great Cairo at leisure. The amiable Maya who appeared on the beach, no fools in the face of smiling strangers bearing gifts and weapons, soon lured some of the Spaniards ashore into a fierce ambush from which they barely escaped. Continuing their voyage of discovery, the wounded and wary newcomers sailed farther along the coast, but only by day, and "with the greatest caution."

Neither historians nor archaeologists have been able to pinpoint Great Cairo with certainty. Some place Díaz's sighting on Isla Mujeres, just north of the modern resort of Cancun. Many equate it with the ruins of Ecab, on the mainland farther north. Wherever it was, Great Cairo provided the outsiders with the first hint of a world vastly different from their own. We now know what Córdoba and his men, blinded by the conviction that Europeans were the sole proprietors of civilized life on earth, could not possibly have imagined: that beyond the town they saw lay a varied land teeming with people, and that the Maya who greeted them were merely the most recent actors in a unique drama of human life and civilization that had begun thousands of years before they dropped anchor.

"The Maya," as archaeologist Michael D. Coe of Yale University reminds us, "are hardly a vanished people. . . ." Today more than four million of them speaking 30 or so versions of their own language live in the mountains and plains of an area about half the size of Texas.

Between about A.D. 250 and 900, the span that archaeologists term the Classic Period, ancestors of the Maya mastered the demanding environment of a tropical forest and shaped one of the most remarkable civilizations of antiquity. At its height, Maya society included farmers of uncommon talent, a vigorous nobility, and skilled craftsmen. Their great cities, their architecture, and their art challenged the splendor of the ancient capitals of Asia and Africa. Their intellectual accomplishments in the scribal arts, mathematics, and astronomy rank with those of the Arab and Hindu worlds. And, unlike its counterparts in the Middle East and Egypt, the Maya achievement took place without the aid of the wheel, beasts of burden, or metal tools.

The land of the Maya covers all of the Yucatan Peninsula and its broad southern base, a territory that stretches from the Pacific Ocean northward to the coastline touched by Córdoba's fleet. The Maya area contains two basic landscapes, highland and lowland, and an astonishing variety of environmental localities within each one. The ridges and active volcanoes that define the highlands stretch from Mexico across southern Guatemala into the western portions of Honduras and El Salvador, crowding a narrow lowland band beside the Pacific. The peninsula itself, a great irregular slab of limestone, shapes an expanse of lowland that comprises roughly two-thirds of the whole Maya area. It covers northern Guatemala, Belize, and southeastern Mexico, including the states of Campeche, Quintana Roo, and Yucatan, and parts of Chiapas and Tabasco.

Both the highlands and the lowlands lie well within the tropics where, on average, the rains come only between May and October, and in varying amounts. Most of this bounty falls in the southern lowlands, the heart of the peninsula, where it has helped to create one of earth's great rain forests. In contrast, the scantier rains of the north maintain only a thorny scrub forest in soil that barely coats the porous limestone bedrock.

In 1576, in a forested river valley in the southeastern part of the Maya area, the Spanish official Diego García de Palacio visited Copan, where he found "proud mansions which appear to have belonged to a great city." Much later, in 1848, Modesto Méndez, Chief Magistrate of Guatemala's Peten district, reported the immense ruin of Tikal to the outside world. "The discovery of these palaces, plazas, ditches, statues, and letters in stone and wood, offers an immense field from which the poet and the historian can reap advantage and use, as they must see."

Méndez was right, but even he would have been astonished at the sheer number and variety of people who have sought the secrets of the Maya. Beginning in the early 1800s, hundreds of individuals ranging from the frivolous to the sober, from the eccentric to the ordinary, have worked to solve the mystery of the ruined cities. The key, as we now know, lies in scientific archaeology, yet that did not get under way in the Maya area until the late 1800s, when the discipline was in its infancy. Since then, methods have rapidly improved, and increasing numbers of scholars and lay people have joined the excavators in the quest, including anthropologists, ethnohistorians, geographers, art historians, linguists, and epigraphists. In all, eight generations of experts from many nations have given us the story of people, time, and change in the land of the Maya.

For the sake of convenience, archaeologists divide the story of the Maya into five major time periods. The Preclassic Period, from around 2000 B.C. to A.D. 250, saw not only the earliest recognizable Maya farming settlements scattered over the area, but also the first stirrings of greatness in the massive pyramids that rose above the forest of the southern lowlands beginning about 600 B.C. The Classic Period, between about A.D. 250 and 900, witnessed the high tide of civilization in dozens of prosperous regional capitals throughout the lowlands and, at the end, the sudden collapse of nearly all of them in the south. During the Postclassic Period (A.D. 900 to 1521), the Maya of the northern lowlands continued to thrive, but on a lesser scale and somewhat erratically, as the power of their petty competing states shifted from capital to capital through an era of rapid change that ended with the

GULF OF

BAY OF

▲ Teotihuacan

★ Mexico City
(Site of
Tenochtitlan)

▲ Cacaxtla

● Veracruz

V E R A C R U Z

M E X I

Las Limas ●

● Oaxaca

O A X A C A

The Maya World

A varied heartland known as Mesoamerica nurtured magnificent ancient cultures. In an area stretching from north-central Mexico as far south as Costa Rica, simple agricultural people shared basic religious ideas and life-styles as early as 2000 B.C. The Olmec, the Zapotec, the builders of Teotihuacan, the Mixtec, the Aztec, and dozens of other societies developed here. By 1500 B.C., local cultures had crystallized, and chiefs ruled modest realms from burgeoning towns. This period, which scholars call the Preclassic, saw the rise of Maya civilization in the southern highlands and in lowlands that stretched northward through the Yucatan Peninsula and along Pacific, Gulf, and Caribbean coasts. In the Classic Period, beginning about A.D. 250, divine kings reigned over powerful city-states,

bringing those in the southern lowlands, such as Tikal, Yaxchilan, and Copan, to fruition. The Classic Maya achieved distinction in many intellectual pursuits— including writing and devising a calendar—but southern lowland

cities had failed by 900. The following Postclassic Period brought religious and political changes and a power shift to cities like Chichen Itza and Tulum on the Yucatan Peninsula. It all ended with the Spanish conquest.

Isla Cerritos ▲
Ecab ▲

YUCATAN

Sisal ●
Isla Mujeres ~
Cancun ●

Komchen ▲   ▲ **Dzibilchaltun**

Merida ●   **Izamal** ●   **Chichen** ● **Itza**   **Balankanche Cave** ▲

Acanceh ●

Mayapan ▲   **Telchaquillo** ●   **Valladolid** ●

Yaxuna ▲   **Dzitnup Cenote**   **Coba** ▲

Ticul ●
P
Mani ●

Uxmal ▲   **Oxkutzcab** ●

Jaina ▲   **Kabah** ▲   *U*   **Tulum** ▲
Sayil ▲   **Loltun Cave**
Labna ▲   *C*
Cozumel Island

Campeche ●

Edzna ▲   *YUCATAN PENINSULA*

QUINTANA ROO

M E X I C O

C A M P E C H E

Xicalango ●   *Laguna de Terminos*

C A M P E C H E

Becan ▲   *Chetumal Bay*

Chicanna ▲   **Chetumal** ●

Rio Bec ▲

Comalcalco ▲   **Kohunlich** ▲   **Cerros** ▲

Calakmul ▲   **Cuello** ▲

T A B A S C O

Balancan ●   **El Mirador** ▲▲   **Rio Azul** ▲   **Lamanai** ▲
Nakbe ▲

Palenque ▲   *Usumacinta R.*   **Uaxactun** ▲   **Barton Ramie** ▲

P E T E N   **Tikal** ▲   **Holmul** ▲

Piedras Negras ▲   **Naranjo** ▲   **Buenavista del Cayo** ▲

Naja ●   **San Jose** ●   ★ **Belmopan**

C   *O*   *Lake Peten Itza*   **Flores (Site of Tayasal)**

San Juan Chamula ●   **Tenejapa** ●   **Tonina** ▲   **Yaxchilan** ▲   **Caracol** ▲

Zinacantan ●   **Corozal** ▲   *BELIZE*

San Cristobal de las Casas ●   **Bonampak** ▲   *Glover Reef*

C H I A P A S   *Lacantun R.*   **Dos Pilas** ▲   *Bay Islands*

Naj Tunich ▲   *GULF OF HONDURAS*

Dulce R. ↓

Nito ▲

G U A T E M A L A   **Naco** ▲

Todos Santos ●   **Quirigua** ▲

Huehuetenango ●   **Nebaj** ●   **San Juan Chamelco** ●   *Motagua R.*

Momostenango ●   **Copan** ●

Quiche ●   **Joyabaj** ●   **Jocotan** ●   *Copan R.*

San Andres Xecul ●   **Chichicastenango** ●

Quezaltenango ●   **Solola** ●

Zunil ●   **Iximche** ▲   *HONDURAS*

Lake Atitlan   ★ **Guatemala City**

Santiago Atitlan   **San Antonio** ●

Antigua Guatemala   **Tegucigalpa** ★

P A C I F I C   O C E A N   *E L   S A L V A D O R*

Tazumal ▲

Ceren ▲

★ **San Salvador**

Scale:
0 — 50 — 100 — 150 MI
0 — 50 — 100 — 150 KM

▲ Site
● Town
▬ Mexican state

appearance of the Spaniards and the conquest of Mexico by Hernán Cortés.

The Colonial Period (1521-1821) brought the holocaust of the conquest to the entire Maya area in a series of terrible military campaigns that began in the highlands in 1524 and ended with the conquest of Yucatan in 1547. The last independent Maya group fell to the Spanish crown in the heart of the southern lowlands in 1697. The Modern Period (1821 to the present) saw some tenacious Maya, goaded beyond even their ability to endure oppression, rise in bloody rebellion against the newcomers, only to be suppressed once more. The Maya of today endure as the largest single group of native Americans north of Peru.

As scholars are continually reminded by their findings, the course of ancient Maya culture took place within the greater context of a region that reaches from north-central Mexico to Costa Rica. The anthropologists call it Mesoamerica and define it not by national boundaries but instead by the fundamental cultural similarity shared by the various Indian societies who lived there. This essential sameness is apparent in ways that range from corn farming to the calendar, and visible in the pyramids, palaces, and plazas that mark archaeological sites from Teotihuacan in Mexico to Tazumal in El Salvador. "It would seem," says archaeologist Arthur Demarest of Vanderbilt University, "that at any given time practically everybody in Mesoamerica knew exactly what everyone else was doing and thinking."

Beneath this unity, and despite it, lay a dazzling variety of languages, art styles, and other regional expressions manifest in the Olmec, the Zapotec, the society that built Teotihuacan, the Mixtec, the Aztec, and dozens of other peoples who rose and fell on the Mesoamerican landscape. The Maya are just one of these, and their story, like that of any who play the game of successful survival on our planet, holds lessons essential to us all.

Today we know even more about the Maya accomplishment than ever before, yet we have barely scratched the surface of their world. Of the nearly 3,500 archaeological sites officially recorded in the highlands and lowlands, only a relative handful have been investigated in more than a cursory fashion, and the number of new sites grows each time a new survey reaches print. One of those in the grand inventory is surely Great Cairo itself, once a living town of real people who loved and laughed and cried. Now it appears to us much as it did to Bernal Díaz del Castillo—a receding mirage that played but a fleeting part in human history. For me, the elusive reality of Great Cairo, trivial as it may seem in the grander sweep of the Maya epic, serves as a constant reminder of the many secrets that still lie hidden in the land.

Olmec youth from Las Limas in Veracruz, Mexico, cradles a divine jaguar-human baby. Thriving from 1200 to 400 B.C., the Olmec established patterns of Mesoamerican culture.

Manuscript scribed in stone: Risers of the Hieroglyphic Stairway at Copan tell of the city's past. Accompanied by dates and names, an honored ancestor lies among some 1,300 glyphs that adorn the stairway, the longest ancient text yet found in the New World. Dates of the glyphs range from A.D. 553 to 751. A ruler named Smoke Shell affirmed the city's greatness by building the stairway to honor his dynastic ancestors after Ruler 18 Rabbit was beheaded by enemies.

RICHARD ALEXANDER COOKE III; KENNETH GARRETT (FOLLOWING PAGES)

FOLLOWING PAGES: Tiers rise to the Temple of the Inscriptions at Palenque in Mexico. In 1952 excavations here revealed, for the first time, that such structures can conceal the tombs of Maya elite. This one held the remains of a seventh-century ruler named Pacal. The Temple of the Cross, atop a partially exposed pyramid, honors his son and successor.

*B*uoyed by long tradition, highland Maya move through today's world. Bright ribbons cascade from the hats of youths from Zinacantan in Mexico's Chiapas state, recalling the plumed headdresses worn by Maya elite. Adjusting to mountain chill (opposite), a woman of nearby Tenejapa matches a warm Western-style sweater with a traditional wraparound skirt. Her companion wears a brocaded blouse unique to her village. In subtle design variations, highland weavers identify their villages and reaffirm their faith in ancient gods of nature.

DISCOVERY

Vuulted room tops a mound in the Puuc region of Yucatan. Word of "stone houses" deep in the forest emerged in mid-18th century; scores of sites await investigation.

In the humid haze of a tropical autumn morning, John Lloyd Stephens and his companions forded the shallow, stony river on mule back and followed a slick trail to the base of an old stone wall, where they dismounted. Entering a dense, gloomy forest, they paused in wonderment at sculptures protruding from the leaves among the trees; then, followed by the rustle of curious spider monkeys in the dark foliage above, they climbed an ancient stone stairway and found themselves in the courtyard of a vast and mysterious acropolis.

"It lay before us like a shattered bark in the midst of the ocean, her masts gone, her name effaced, her crew perished, and none to tell whence she came, to whom she belonged, how long on her voyage, or what caused her destruction."

Stephens, a New York lawyer turned successful travel writer, and his colleague, British artist Frederick Catherwood, had come to Central America because of some books they had perused in New York only months before. The works had reported three obscure ruins—"stone houses," one said—in the Mexican and Central American hinterland: Palenque, Uxmal, and Copan. As Stephens put it with typical understatement, they "roused our curiosity." In the autumn of 1839, when they stood in awe amid the fallen buildings of Copan, Stephens and Catherwood had begun the most remarkable journey ever taken through the Maya world. In two separate expeditions completed in 1842, they traveled the Maya area on foot, by mule, and in dugout canoe. Plagued by illness and the perils of ongoing civil war and often guided only by local hearsay, they managed to visit most of the now-famous cities of the ancient Maya—Copan, Quirigua, Palenque, Uxmal, Chichen Itza, Tulum, and many others as well. "In our long, irregular, and devious route," wrote Stephens, "we have discovered the crumbling remains of forty-four ancient cities. . . . with but few exceptions, all were lost, buried and unknown, never before visited by a stranger. . . ."

Unlike his predecessors, John Lloyd Stephens correctly believed that the Maya themselves were responsible for the cities he had seen, and speculated with instinctive logic that the hieroglyphs carved on the stones dealt with the history of their kings. As for the date, the origin, and the fate of the Maya cities, and other questions invoked by the fallen stones, Stephens said it best: "All was mystery, dark, impenetrable mystery. . . ." Even as he pondered the riddle of the ruins, clues of another kind had begun to surface on both sides of the Atlantic. In the local archives of Yucatan, scholar Juan Pío Pérez had found a cache of Colonial Period documents written in Mayan, but in the alphabet of the conquerors. These contained snatches of remembered history, astrology, and prophecy, often keyed to what was left of the old calendar.

In the parish archives of a church in present-day Chichicastenango, Guatemala, a friar found a 16th-century manuscript in Quiche Mayan, titled the Popol Vuh, or Council Book. A treasure trove of highland Maya mythology and history, it ranks among the greatest works of native American literature.

In 1863, the tireless French cleric Brasseur de Bourbourg, who had already helped to bring the Popol Vuh to European readers, made another miraculous discovery. In Madrid, he came upon a copy of the long-lost *Relación de las Cosas de Yucatan*, or "Account of the Affairs of Yucatan." Composed some 300 years earlier by Friar Diego de Landa, later Bishop of Yucatan, the document provided a first-hand look at northern Maya society in the decade immediately after the conquest.

In the 1880s, Englishman Alfred Percival Maudslay carried the search back into the Maya area. Following the trails of Stephens and Catherwood and others, he compiled a compendium of ancient Maya buildings, sculptures, and hieroglyphic texts—a unique and lasting gift to Maya scholarship. By 1892, publication of ancient Maya materials had reached a kind of critical mass. Three Maya codices— or books—that had ended up in Dresden, Paris, and Madrid were available, along with a sample of the chronicles of ancient Yucatan, the Popol Vuh, the Landa account and, of course, the ruins themselves. As Mexican scholar Ignacio Bernal put it, "the pace of work was heating up, and foundations were being laid. . . ."

Scientific excavation of Maya sites began at Copan in the 1890s under the auspices of Harvard University's Peabody Museum and matured in 1912 at Holmul, Guatemala, where Raymond Merwin carefully exposed successive layers of construction and recognized their differences in age. Maya archaeology accelerated after World War I under the enthusiastic guidance of Sylvanus G. Morley and the Carnegie Institution of Washington, D.C. Between 1924 and 1958, a span that still stands for many as a golden age of Maya investigation, a succession of Carnegie scholars converged on the Maya world. While the Carnegie investigators gathered information on every conceivable Maya topic from modern folk medicine and body measurements to hieroglyphic decipherment and history, teams from Tulane University, the British Museum, and others mapped, dug, and described new ruins from the Lacandon forest to the interior of Belize.

In the meantime, nearly two decades of exploration in the Maya area by Mexico's National Institute of Anthropology and History (INAH) culminated in 1952 with Alberto Ruz's unprecedented discovery of a spectacular royal crypt deep beneath the Temple of the Inscriptions at Palenque. The University Museum of Archaeology and Anthropology in Philadelphia devoted the 1930s to the exploration of Piedras Negras, and in 1956 began a massive archaeological project at Tikal in cooperation with Guatemalan scientists.

Since its beginning, Maya archaeology has changed much as did the culture it seeks to expose. If we had to divide the evolution of the discipline into periods, we might use the perfect vision of hindsight to select 1960 as a convenient point at which to mark the boundary between traditional Maya archaeology and the present form of the science.

During the period of traditional archaeology, a fundamental Maya chronology emerged, thanks to the layers of ceramics found at Uaxactun and other sites, the development of radiocarbon dating, and the understanding of the calendar used in the codices and the carvings. By 1960, however, out of the hundreds of glyphic texts, only the dates could be read with certainty, so the Maya seemed a people obsessed with time. And since the archaeologists had, in general, mapped or excavated only the largest buildings at each site, the ancient Maya appeared to emerge as a civilization without cities. The Maya, thought many, consisted of a peaceful society of peasants and a priestly nobility of contemplative astronomers living in the shadow of empty "ceremonial centers" maintained by caretaker priests concerned mainly with the gods and the movement of the heavens. And, agreed most, they apparently achieved greatness in almost total isolation, unaffected by their neighbors. In short, before about 1960, the ancient Maya were perceived as a people unlike any other known to have ever existed.

Our image of the builders of the ancient cities has changed dramatically since 1960. Some of the reasons lie in the flood of hieroglyphic decipherments pioneered by epigraphists Yuri Knorozov, Heinrich Berlin, and Tatiana Proskouriakoff. These show that the inscriptions deal largely with the lives and careers of the rulers and members of their courts. In archaeology, a host of new conclusions have come about through thorough mapping and improved methods of sampling the sites. Settlement studies, pioneered by Harvard's Gordon R. Willey at Barton Ramie, Belize, now embrace not only the great "downtown" palaces and pyramids but the less spectacular remains of outlying suburbs as well. The University Museum's detailed map of Tikal, for example, helps us to see it as a teeming city of perhaps 55,000 people in the Late Classic Period. Excavations, which sampled all parts of Tikal, have helped to reveal a society much more complex than anyone could have imagined before.

The process of trying to know, understand, and explain the ancient Maya will probably never end. Refined techniques in remote sensing by satellites are even now revising our view of the relationship between the ancient Maya and their environment in terms of the changes that seem to have taken place in both. Meanwhile, continuing decipherments of the old texts, now becoming available on computer data bases, help us look into the very minds of the makers of the cities Stephens found.

The story of the discovery of the Maya comes full circle at Copan. There, nearly two decades of intensive investigation of the city and its valley, supervised by the Honduran Institute of Anthropology and History, have revealed many of the secrets of its people and the 16 kings who ruled them for 400 years. In the East Court of the Acropolis, near the spot where John Lloyd Stephens contemplated the dark mystery of the fallen stones 150 years ago, one can now almost hear the ancient human sounds of the city as they rise to vanquish the silence.

Gigantic stucco face, reclaimed by the jungle, peers from dense foliage at Piedras Negras. Discovered in the 1930s, the mask once glowered from a pyramid's terraced walls.

*W*ith rope and pulley, workers shore up the face of the Acropolis at Copan (right). Centuries of erosion by the Copan River have cut away the eastern side of the complex, revealing an accumulation of structures. Exposed plaster floors and masonry walls 600 feet long and 131 feet high record a history of 400 years of construction. In 1839, when explorer John Lloyd Stephens saw Copan, "All was mystery, dark, impenetrable mystery. . . ." Some 50 years later, Harvard University's Peabody Museum undertook large-scale excavation at the site, clearing rubble from structures and mapping them. In the 1930s, scientists from the Carnegie Institution of Washington, D.C., diverted the river to avoid further damage. Below, straining workers at Copan lift the capstone off a royal tomb, the first discovered in a century of exploration. It held a scribe, son of the city's greatest king. Such work by scholars has made Copan one of the most thoroughly investigated of Maya sites.

KENNETH GARRETT (BOTH)

34

Mayanists probe the past to reconstruct a lost civilization. Artist Barbara Fash and conservator Rufino Membreño clean a floor carving discovered at Copan in 1992. Sculptured for the dedication of a dynastic temple, it was unearthed from beneath the Hieroglyphic Stairway. Project director William L. Fash calls it the "cornerstone of Copan," for it established Copan as a royal ceremonial center. Blackened remains of featherwork lay atop the stone, probably placed there as an offering. Carved on the weathered marker (below), two rulers holding symbols of authority and wearing splendid headdresses sit facing a row of glyphs. The figure on the left is the founder of the dynasty of 16 kings that sustained Copan's greatness for almost 400 years; the other figure may be his son and successor, Mat Head. Newly deciphered glyphs and dramatic finds in tombs give names and dates of Copan rulers. Similarly, studies of settlement patterns provide insight into suburbs and the people who labored there to support the lords of Copan.

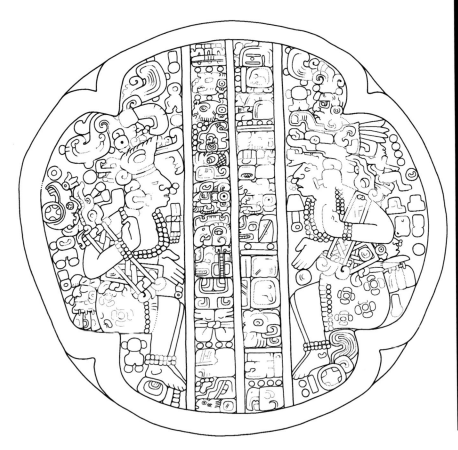

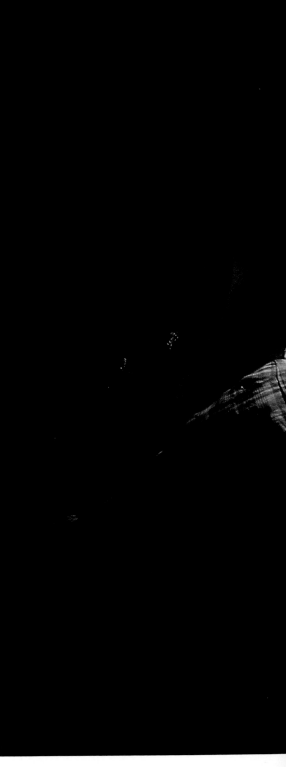

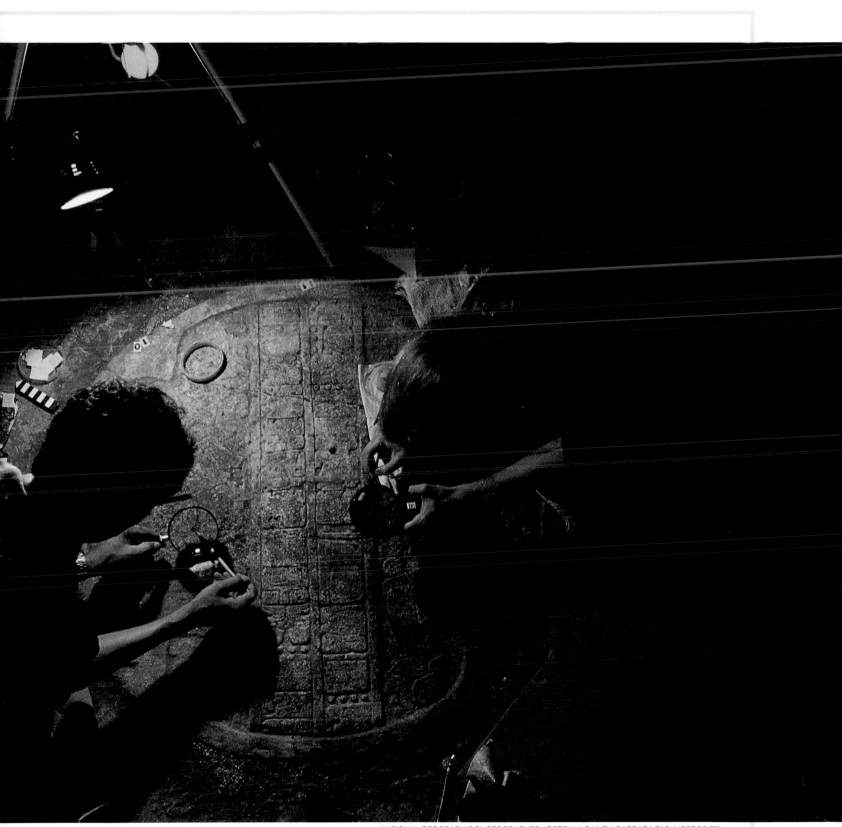

"PROUD MANSIONS":
Frederick Catherwood

"He was standing with his feet in the mud, and was drawing with his gloves on, to protect his hands from the moschetoes," recalled John Lloyd Stephens of a humid, oppressive November morning in 1839. His artist-companion, Frederick Catherwood, stood in despondent bewilderment, attempting in vain to capture the intricate detail of a carved Copan stela.

At the time, Frederick Catherwood was 40 years old. Born in London, he had studied classical art and architecture and traveled widely between 1821 and 1836 in Italy, Greece, Egypt, and the Middle East. Returning to London, Catherwood soon became involved in the exhibition of a great panoramic painting of Jerusalem, and there met Stephens. On September 9, 1839, they signed a contract to explore together the ancient cities of Central America.

The problem Catherwood faced was not a new one. Earlier illustrators of Maya sculptures, educated in classical European art, had unwittingly transferred the styles of ancient Greece and Rome to their drawings. Not so Catherwood. With the help of his own persistence and a camera lucida that allowed him to project the images directly onto paper, he became the first artist to overcome the Maya style barrier. He went on to produce hundreds of drawings and paintings of ancient Maya art and architecture with unprecedented accuracy.

Catherwood the man remains largely an enigma. His only known portrait, incorporated into one of his own views, shows him as a distant, blurry figure helping to measure a temple. In a chain of misfortunes that began immediately after the Maya travels, Catherwood lost most of his life's work—and the painting of Jerusalem as well—in a fire that consumed the New York Panorama building on July 31, 1842.

The legacy of this unknown and largely unsung hero consists of a few sketches and watercolors, the 200 or so engravings that fill Stephens's books, and 25 superb hand-colored lithographs of Maya ruins issued in 1844.

Catherwood spent the last few years of his life as a civil engineer and surveyor for railroad construction in South America, Panama, and California. His death at sea, in the 1854 sinking of the S.S. *Arctic* in the North Atlantic, received only a single laconic line in the press weeks after the tragedy: "Mr. Catherwood Also Is Missing."

Richly detailed lithographs by Frederick Catherwood brought Maya ruins to life. Here, Indians examine a serpent killed at the House of the Governor in Uxmal.

FROM "VIEWS OF ANCIENT MONUMENTS IN CENTRAL AMERICA, CHIAPAS, AND YUCATAN," FREDERICK CATHERWOOD, 1844

ANCIENT MAYA

Temple of the Seven Dolls at Dzibilchaltun, one of the major sites of Yucatan,
probably served as a center for Classic Period solar rituals.

Coral islets of Glover Reef off Belize evoke a Maya view of earth's origins: At the gods' command, land appeared like a creature rising from the sea. A detail from a Maya-style mural at

Cacaxtla in central Mexico (opposite) illustrates an explanation of human origins: After first failing with animals, clay, and wood, the gods finally fashioned people from corn.

FOLLOWING PAGES: In Yucatan a shaman invokes blessings on the harvest. His altar reflects the Maya four-sided earth; the Christian cross doubles as their sacred tree of life.

KENNETH GARRETT; ENRICO FERORELLI (OPPOSITE); DAVID ALLEN HARVEY (PRECEDING AND FOLLOWING PAGES)

A COSMIC VIEW

by Gene S. Stuart

might be inhabited by a spirit; deities could live in the depths of mountains. Along with predatory jaguars and deadly serpents, ghosts prowled the night; spirits roamed the forests, wafting with eerie danger on certain ill winds.

All things joined in a unity of life, in a communion, each a part of the other. It is said that a hunter in Yucatan would appease the god who protected deer with an offering of corn gruel, explaining his aggression to his fallen prey—"I had need." The Maya went beyond sharing the physical world with animals. Humans, they believed, had animal "co-essences." A ruler's creature-companion was the jaguar. William L. Fash, of Northern Illinois University and Director of the Acropolis Archaeological Project at Copan, writes: "The jaguar was considered to be the intermediary between the world of the living and the world of the dead, and a protector and symbol for the Classic Maya royal houses." In 1988, excavations next to Altar Q at Copan, which portrays 16 kings of the royal dynasty, revealed an astonishing find: In A.D. 775, 15 jaguars had been sacrificed by the ruler Yax Pac and buried in a masonry crypt—a jaguar for each of his royal ancestors.

Two of the most sacred features of the landscape served as transitions between the physical world and the spirit world. These were mountains and caves, a Mesoamerican concept already ancient when Maya culture developed. Some symbols on temples and pyramids proclaim them man-made mountains and centers of power. And a temple doorway represented a cave leading into the center of that mountain—and into the Underworld. The Maya believed the entrance to the Underworld lay in the gaping maw of the reptilian earth-creature, and they likened the mouths of caves to it. Visit one of these mystical thresholds and you understand the Maya concept. In a searing and brilliant tropical noon, the chasm leading into Yucatan's Loltun Cave yawns with the rush of sudden and silent cold air, like exhalations from the dead. Ever-darkening tunnels lead downward and into a world of no light, hidden chambers, astounding stalactites and stalagmites, and water.

In the northern highlands, rivers often rush through mountain valleys only to disappear suddenly into an enormous earthen mouth. A network of underground rivers flows in unending darkness. Through black streams and in cave pools swim pale fish without color and with atrophied eyes. Shrimps, sightless and startlingly transparent, feel their way through liquid depths, searching. In the mountains of Guatemala, modern Maya still call one fearsome cave Xibalba.

The Popol Vuh recounts the story of twins who journeyed to Xibalba. For the Maya, their round of adventures serves as a metaphor for timeless, repeating cycles and for the regeneration of earth and all living things.

With gap-toothed countenance, an ageless god—one of four believed to hold up the sky—inhabits Copan. Behind him rises a ceiba, the sacred World Tree thought to unite the universe.

*T*oil-worn hands reverently cradle ears of corn—"God's holy sunbeams." The agricultural foundation of Mesoamerican cultures, corn was being grown in the Maya area by 2000 B.C. The Maya believe that corn—like all plants—has an inner life and soul. During earthquakes, highland farmers call out to the corn in their fields to comfort the disturbed plants. Each step of the cultivation, harvest, and ritual consumption of corn has long been a sacred duty. Men plant and tend the divine crop; women prepare it. At left, corn tortillas, tomatoes, and a chili pepper cook on a griddle over an open fire.

51

Companion creatures in a sacred universe, many animals held mystical meaning for the ancient Maya. Jaguars— kings of the forest—served as "co-essences" for divine rulers. In myth, howler monkey twins became gods of scribes, and in art depicting ceremonies and rituals, snakes often appear.

FOLLOWING PAGES: Caves and natural wells, such as the Cenote of Dzitnup in Yucatan, led to the Maya Underworld, the dreaded, watery realm of death.

A COSMIC VIEW:

The Hero Twins

In another age, in a time of myth and magic, twin brothers called Hunahpu and Xbalanque played ball near the edge of the Great Abyss. The dreaded Lords of Xibalba, or the Underworld, heard the boys' boisterous game. "They are hereby summoned," the lords told their messengers. So the twins descended the face of a cliff into the place of evil, pestilence, and horror. The lords had already killed the father and uncle of Hunahpu and Xbalanque—also twins—who had journeyed to that fearsome realm and never returned.

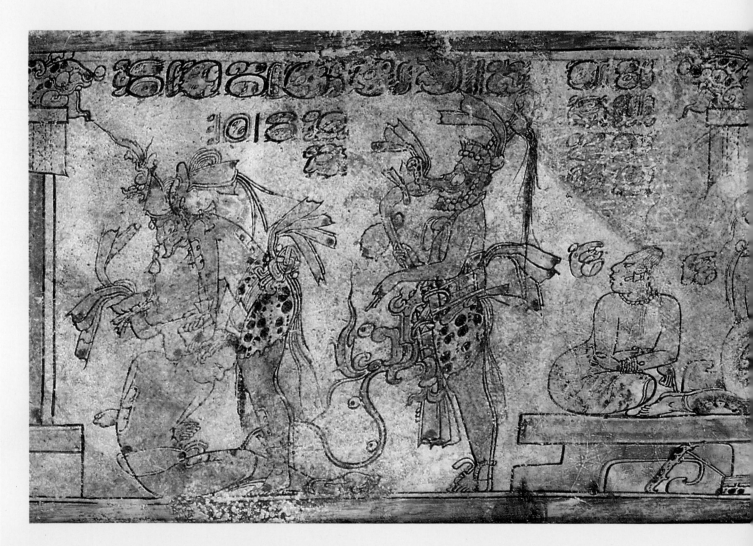

Wondrous exploits of the mythical Hero Twins, on the left, unfold in a photographic rollout, which

But Hunahpu and Xbalanque were resourceful and cunning in escaping from traps and in fulfilling the tasks the lords gave them. Their first night in Xibalba they entered Dark House. Challenged to keep a flaming torch and two cigars burning through the night, the twins attached red macaw plumes to the torch and tipped their cigars with glowing fireflies. The next day they deliberately lost an Underworld ball game, as well as the bet on it—which was to present four bowls filled with flowers to the victors by morning. Leaf-cutting ants summoned by the twins worked through the night gathering the blossoms—from the lords' own gardens. The twins spent that night in Razor House, a structure filled with sharp, moving knives; they promised animal flesh to the voracious stone blades and stilled them.

As the trials continued, the boys appeased the fierce animals of Jaguar House with bones, causing the Xibalbans to think the jaguars had eaten the pair. A burning house only toasted the brothers. Finally, disguised as ragged vagabonds and unrecognized, the twins danced, sang, and performed miracles in Xibalba, and the lords commanded the two strangers to entertain them. Fascinated, they watched the boys sacrifice a dog and then bring it back to life. On command, they did the same to a human. "Sacrifice yet again, even do it to yourselves!" the excited lords said, and they did. "Do it to us!" cried the ruler, One Death, and a lord named Seven Death. So Hunahpu and Xbalanque obliged: The ruler and the lord did not come back to life. The triumphant twins told the surviving lords—"makers of enemies, users of owls . . . masters of hidden intentions"—that from that time Xibalba would hold only violent, worthless, and guilty humans.

The brothers then ascended from Xibalba. Now one twin shines as the sun, the other is the moon, and the Four Hundred Boys, previously slain gods, "became the sky's own stars."

JUSTIN KERR

renders a cylindrical vase as a flat photograph.

57

*R*ising above Guatemala's lowland rain forest, the bones of ancient Tikal pierce the morning fog. The city flourished from about 300 B.C. to A.D. 900. At its height in the eighth century, it covered 50 square miles—a bustling metropolis of perhaps 55,000 people and 3,000 major structures. A toddler (opposite), slung from her mother's back, rides toil-free.

FOLLOWING PAGES: Highland villagers arrayed in traditionally vivid colors and bold patterns brighten the crowded streets of Huehuetenango in Guatemala.

THE
CITIES

by George E. Stuart

among the Puuc cities than had previously existed in the lowlands."

Unfortunately, this brilliant constellation of cities amid the hills of southwestern Yucatan did not endure. Perhaps population simply overcame its once-rich soil and the supply of water. With the abandonment of the Puuc region by about 1000, the epic of Maya cities moved into its final stage, the Postclassic, and to the thriving city of Chichen Itza.

Linked by its port town at Isla Cerritos to the Gulf and Caribbean canoe trade, and perhaps bolstered by rulership freed of the dynastic style of the Classic Period, cosmopolitan Chichen Itza appears to have dominated much of the north before falling amid the bickering politics of 12th-century Yucatan. In its stead rose Mayapan, whose layout consists of 4,000 structures, including about 140 ceremonial buildings, densely packed inside a thick stone wall. The time of troubled power ended for this last Maya capital around 1450, less than a hundred years before the Spaniards began to impose their own city grids on the landscape.

Even in desolation and ruin, the ancient Maya cities continue to surprise the archaeologists. At Nakbe in Guatemala, Richard D. Hansen of UCLA has pushed the Maya beginnings at least to the fourth century B.C. with his dating of a gigantic platform decorated with the huge stucco head of a supernatural bird. And only recently, William Folan and his team from the University of Campeche, Mexico, completed the first detailed map of Calakmul, a sleeping giant of a place near the geographical heart of the Yucatan Peninsula. To the astonishment of practically everyone but himself, it graphically demonstrates that those ruins now rank as one of the largest of all ancient Maya cities. He is proud of his accomplishment but modest. "No bells, no whistles," he said, the first time he showed me the new map, dense with the patterns of pyramids, palaces, and habitations. "Obviously, we've still got a lot to do."

While visiting Calakmul not long ago, I followed the long, steep trail that leads up Structure 2, one of the pair of immense mounds that rise like twin islands in an endless ocean of dark green treetops. Its summit is silent except for bird cries and the ruffle of wind making waves in the forest below, and the view commands an area approximately the size of Delaware. Within the visible horizon, according to a reconnaissance map made in the 1930s, at least a dozen ancient Maya cities lie in the shadows beneath the canopy, waiting to add their chapters to the story. Willie Folan is right—we've still got a lot to do.

Archaeological assistant Mario Coyoc examines pottery fragments in a royal tomb at Calakmul, once one of the largest cities on the Yucatan Peninsula in both size and population.

FOLLOWING PAGES: Like mountains in miniature, the ruins of Maya pyramids at Tonina in Chiapas, Mexico, reflect the nature of the sacred land from which they spring.

*T*unnel to the heart of a Maya pyramid reveals a surprise: In 1989, archaeologists at Copan discovered, entombed within a pyramid, a hidden, smaller temple (right) that had survived undamaged and unplundered for some 1,400 years—the only known example of an intact Maya structure at the site. Here, team leader Ricardo Agurcia Fasquelle of the Honduran Institute of Anthropology and History examines a corner exposed when workers removed rubble from between the buildings. The figure in the niche may have honored a royal Maya ancestor. Dubbed Rosalila, the entire temple measures about 55 by 40 feet and stands above the ruins of even earlier structures. Below, a modeled stucco sculpture on the temple probably represents a primordial deity.

69

Archaeologist William Fash (standing), project artist Barbara Fash, and Rudy Larios, in charge of restoration, inspect the upper facade of a building at Copan. The woven-mat stonework pattern identifies the structure as popol nah—or Mat House—a community council house. Here the ruler and his nobles met to carry out day-to-day administrative duties and to take part in ritual dances and celebrations. The fish-shaped hieroglyph above the pillar represents a place-name. The building dates from the eighth century A.D. and the 11-year reign of Smoke Monkey. Two-foot-high ceramic effigy figures, pieced together from fragments found outside the tomb of a royal scribe in Copan, perch atop the lids of incense burners.

KENNETH GARRETT (BOTH)

71

GUILLERMO ALDANA E.

72

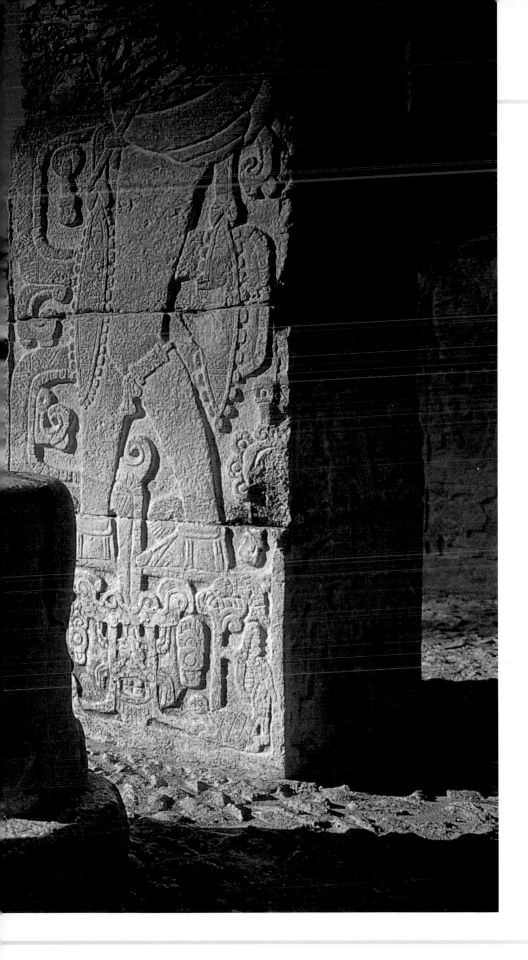

*J*aguar-shaped throne of stone
turns its sightless gaze toward
the Castillo, a pyramid
dominating the skyline at
Chichen Itza in northern
Yucatan. On a column beside the
throne stands a warrior bearing a
shield. Such Toltec motifs
mingled with earlier Maya
pyramidal structures and
provided a cosmopolitan flair to
this Postclassic city, which rose to
power sometime after A.D. 800.
For about 300 years after the
collapse of more southerly
lowland cities such as Tikal and
Palenque, Chichen Itza ranked
first among a constellation of
northern lowland centers of
commerce and religion. Then it
too faded from glory, succumbing
to the political bickering and
fighting that rattled through the
peninsula in the 12th century.

*O*ne of the last outposts of
Maya civilization, Tulum
thrived as a religious and trading

center for seagoing Maya
merchants from about A.D. 1200
until the conquest. Canoes landed
at a beach within its walls. The
Castillo, some 40 feet high, still
provides a landmark along the
Caribbean coast of the peninsula
and dominates the colonnaded
ruins of a once bustling plaza.

Fit for a king—and for his extended family as well—the Great Palace at Sayil in Yucatan grew to three stories and nearly a hundred rooms between A.D. 750 and 900. In a society of mutual *dependence, kings reigned with guidance from the gods and support from the masses. An elite matron (opposite), a clay figurine from Chiapas, calmly controls a dog and a toddler.* *FOLLOWING PAGES: Citizens from Todos Santos in Guatemala gather to welcome home exiles from Mexico. A yearly festival here marks the town's namesake holiday, All Saints' Day.*

THE PEOPLE

by Gene S. Stuart

*A*rrayed in ritual attire, modeled clay figurines from Jaina Island off the Campeche coast reveal a variety of upper-class personages from the Late Classic Period. A warrior dressed for battle wears a cumbersome headdress. In one hand he carries his rectangular shield, tufted with feathers. His tunic of padded cotton armor will help protect him in conflicts; from it protrude what may be cacao pods. Rulers and other lords led troops into battle, becoming sacrificial victims at the hands of rival kings when defeated. Women, themselves sometimes rulers, played pivotal religious and social roles. Royal marriages between lineages of city-states sealed political alliances and could increase the prestige of both parties. A woman (opposite, upper) wears wide bracelets and a necklace of large shell or stone beads; a traditional Mesoamerican garment falls fetchingly from her shoulders.

Coiffures often became works of art in themselves: Beneath a smooth, upswept crest, this woman's hair is trimmed in sharp angles around her face. At right, a man, possibly taking part in a religious ritual, gracefully balances a huge deer headdress as he smokes a cigar. Tobacco, a sacred plant to the Maya, was used to induce visions.

JUSTIN KERR (ALL)

*T*wo weavers in timeless motion: María Pérez of San Antonio, Guatemala, kneeling at a backstrap loom, has just inserted the weft; next she will strike home the thread with the batten, as her Late Classic counterpart, modeled in clay from Jaina (below), is doing. María's cotton fabric likely will become her family's clothing, its patterns and styles traditional since Classic times. Wool appears here in the boys' kiltlike hip cloths and María's headband.

*S*alute to a humble home: Part of a facade at Uxmal has a thatched roof mimicked in stone. A modern family's house in Yucatan (opposite) is of a style little changed in more than 3,000 years. Walls may be stone, mud, or lashed saplings. Palm leaves or grasses form well-insulated roofs.

In cold weather—rare on the peninsula—a one-room house's open fire on a dirt floor dispels chills. In the more usual heat, the thatch helps keep the interior cool. The roof's steep pitch diverts the rainy season's heavy downpours.

KENNETH GARRETT; DAVID ALLEN HARVEY (OPPOSITE)

*I*n a centuries-old cycle, farmers in Honduras plant corn. Using planting sticks, they punch holes, drop in several seeds, then cover them—and wait for rain. Turned from the fire and smoke, Mario Antonio Raigosa (opposite) clears brush for a new field near Mani, Yucatan, using the ancient slash-and-burn method of cultivation. Because of the thin topsoil in Yucatan, farmers use a field for two or three years, then let it lie fallow for as many as fifteen. Scholars say ancient Maya farming techniques varied with terrain. The main method was slash-and-burn. In

addition, some highlanders built terraces; lowlanders often dug irrigation canals or constructed raised fields. Forest dwellers planted a mix of crops among fruit-bearing or other useful trees. Many Maya had gardens with foods probably chosen to attract deer and other game.

KENNETH GARRETT; DAVID ALLEN HARVEY (ABOVE)

SOCIETY:
Court Life

With a withering glance and a graceful gesture, a Maya king acknowledges two people who are probably lesser lords in this scene of royal Maya court life. The seated lord presents a jaguar—or its skin—to the ruler, while his kneeling companion urges him on with a surreptitious nudge on his back. Small dots rising from their mouths highlight their spoken words, shown in glyphs as yet undeciphered.

Opulence and elegance abound. The enthroned ruler wears a cape of feathery cutout design. Twists of fine fabrics form turbans from which precious plumes sway. Glyphs and gods adorn the cloth of one.

Such scenes on painted vases, in murals, and in sculpture provide detailed glimpses of court life in the Classic Period.

Some kings and their royal families lived in the luxury of enormous palaces. Other rulers, however, may have lived apart from their wives and children in private apartments or in a house, as archaeologist William T. Sanders of Pennsylvania State University suggests the sacred rulers of Copan perhaps did.

Throughout the Maya area these pampered kings filled their days with divine ritual. At appropriate times they performed bloodletting ceremonies, experienced hallucinogenic trances, and often appeared to the populace in the guise of gods.

For an heir designate, royal routine began at an early age, in part to ensure the chosen succession in the dynasty. Murals at Bonampak picture a poignant ceremony: The ruler is presenting a child-in-arms to his court. On one carved panel from Piedras Negras, a youth and a king, both in fearsome, sacred war regalia, stand in a ritual before a helmeted and kneeling group

who may be the sons of loyal nobility. The ruler, the gods, and the society led lives of complex interdependence.

Royal families included descendants of previous rulers, and by A.D. 800, as the Classic Period slipped into its decline, this most elite hierarchy had grown enormous.

Mary Ellen Miller and Linda Schele hypothesize a dynasty founded by a royal couple about A.D. 600. If that couple had 4 children, and that rate of reproduction followed through 3 generations, and all 16 grandchildren married first cousins, the pair would have 32 great-grandchildren. Given the multiple wives of some kings—which became the custom in some Maya cities—a royal family became an overwhelming burden to the lower classes who had to support it. Miller and Schele write that "following a simple pattern of cross-cousin marriage and a family size limited to four children, within 200 years, or by A.D. 800, the direct descendants of the original couple would number, very conservatively, at least 500 people."

Animated world of the Maya court comes to life in rare murals that survived under a coating of leached limestone in a temple at Bonampak, Mexico. In this copy, a procession heralds the presentation of a child heir to the throne. Musicians blow horns, strike turtle shells and drums, and shake rattles, accompanied by actors clad as bizarre creatures— including a crustacean.

FOLLOWING PAGES: In a macabre vision carved in stucco at Tonina, a skeletal death god named Turtle Foot wears a turtle shell on his instep and hoists a severed head by its hair.

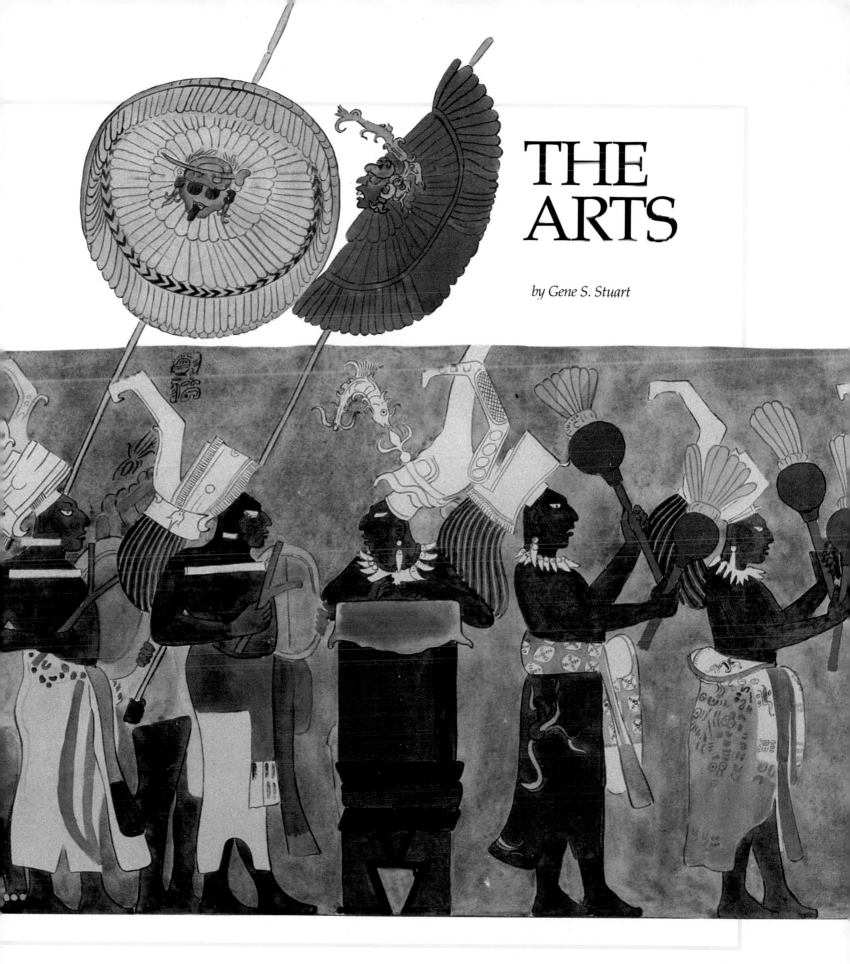

THE
ARTS

by Gene S. Stuart

jade figurines and plaques, often keeping a carving for generations and then making an offering of it, perhaps in a royal tomb. One jade plaque carved about 800 B.C. by the Olmec—esteemed predecessors of the Maya—came to light in a burial on Cozumel Island in Mexico that dated to about A.D. 800. That heirloom, then, had been treasured for 1,600 years or more before it became a funerary gift.

Artifacts of clay are common in Maya art. Both Preclassic and Postclassic artisans produced masterpieces, but here again Classic artists excelled, especially in shaping and decorating vessels. Effigy-pot forms ranged from gods and humans to animals and vegetables. In one technique, artisans carved decorations into pottery when the clay had dried to a leather-hard consistency.

But their painted polychrome vessels are special. Illustrations on cylindrical pots vary from revered deities to court scenes to demonic concepts of the Underworld. Similar paintings showing the supernatural world likely illustrated Classic Maya codices, but unfortunately none of the codices survive. These vessels tell us stories, whether or not they can be read. And some are in styles so distinct that individual artists or workshops can be identified. Many bear the artist's—or owner's—name.

While excavating the ruins of Buenavista del Cayo in Belize in the 1980s, archaeologists Jennifer T. Taschek and Joseph W. Ball of San Diego State University made a surprising discovery in an eighth-century royal crypt. A young lord had been laid to rest dressed in jaguar-skin clothing, complete with mittens made of jaguar paws. Among the high-status offerings placed with him was a valued and inscribed painted vessel showing another young lord—the corn god. The glyphs, deciphered by David Stuart and Stephen D. Houston of Vanderbilt University, read in part, "his drinking vessel for the 'seasoned' cacao," followed by the name "Smoke Squirrel," a well-known ruler of Naranjo, a far more powerful city that lay only eight miles away. Scholars surmise that this vessel, specially made to hold chocolate drinks, had been owned by the esteemed Smoke Squirrel and had been presented as a gift to Buenavista's subordinate—but respected—ruling family.

Portable art in the form of clay figurines often reveals an enchanting and less formal view of Maya life. A treasury of Late Classic funerary gifts in the form of clay figurines comes from Jaina Island on the Yucatan Peninsula's Gulf coast. Subjects include animals and flowers, as well as nobility and gods. One of the most charming shows a deity wearing a tunic of rich design and a massive backrack covered entirely in plumes. His lips are slightly parted as if speaking or singing. Gracefully, he swings one hand up and bends his knees in a sprightly dance. He is a joyful god, a reciter, a great singer and musician. He is Ah Kin Xoc, the god of poetry.

Delicate silhouette, perhaps of a ruler or a deity, emerges in an eccentric flint. Requiring hundreds of hours to create, these rare objects may have capped ceremonial staffs.

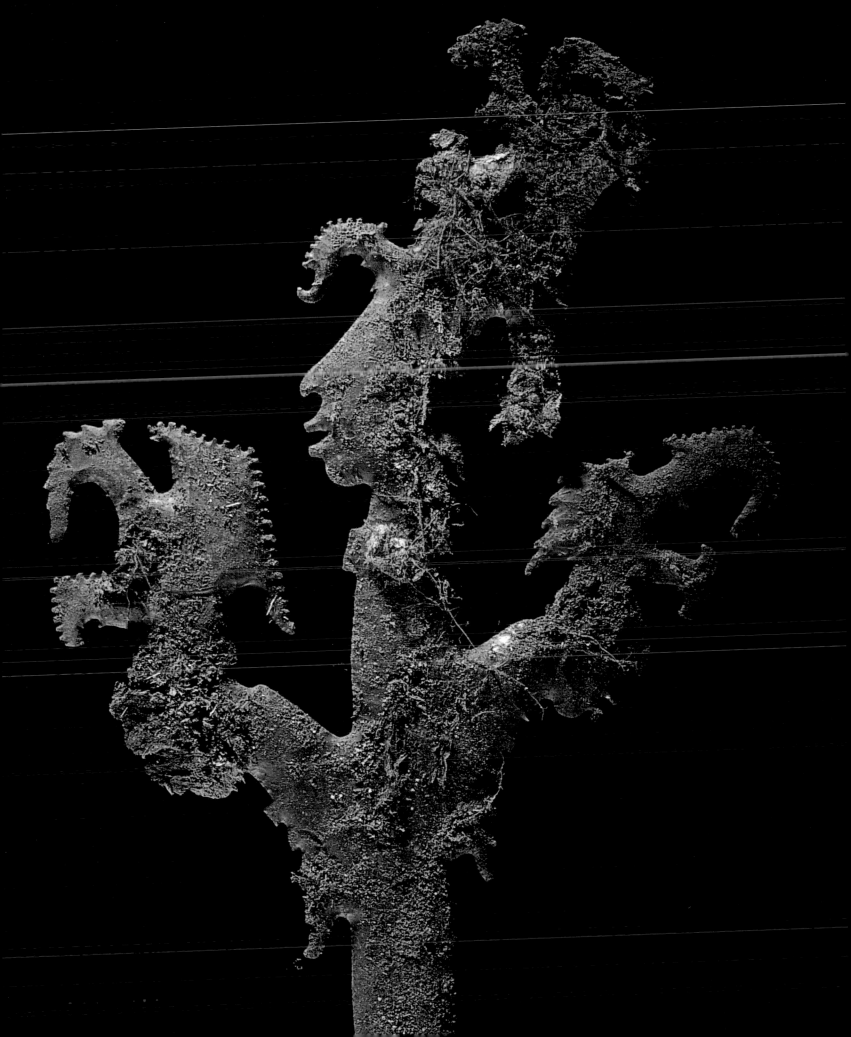

*O*rnate stone stela provides a perfect nesting niche for a great kiskadee at Copan. The eighth-century sculpture portrays the powerful Copan ruler 18 Rabbit, who in his long 43-year reign presided over a major artistic flowering. The deep, almost in the round relief demonstrates a baroque complexity characteristic of the Copan style of the time. The hat of spiraling strips of fabric beneath the ruler's ornate headdress remains standard festive headgear today in parts of Guatemala.

Participants at an Easter procession at Santiago Atitlan in Guatemala (below) wear the same style of colorful, tightly wound woven cloth.

Portrait of a Maya noble: Detail from a carved limestone monument at Balancan, near Palenque, illustrates the ideal of beauty in a young man (opposite). His profile shows a long, sloping forehead produced in infancy by clamping the skull between boards. "Lady Eveningstar let blood," read glyphs inscribed on the eighth-century stela (left) from Yaxchilan, Mexico. In this rare depiction of a woman in monumental Maya art, the mother of the ruler Bird Jaguar holds a bowl filled with strips of paper to catch her own blood, to be spilled in ritual tongue-piercing. Fragile artwork that has not survived—featherwork and textiles, for instance—often appears on such sculptures. Different styles evolved over the Maya area, from the intricate Copan sculpture nearly in the round to the simpler designs in relief shown here. Seeing such work, John Lloyd Stephens concluded that "savages never carved these stones."

*S*unset burnishes the facade of the Palace of the Masks at Kabah in Yucatan, an especially ornate example of the Puuc style of architecture. A curved stone nose (opposite) once protruded from one of some 250 nearly identical masks on the building's 150-foot facade. Most Maya architecture used two basic elements: platforms and roofed rectangles with central doorways.

FOLLOWING PAGES: Caana, a sacred pyramidal complex that encompassed temples, tombs, and living quarters, emerges from the dense rain forest at Caracol, Belize's largest Classic site.

THE BUILDERS

by George E. Stuart

Late on an August evening in or around A.D. 590, a volcano erupted without warning in the tranquil Zapotitan Valley of El Salvador. The episode produced lava bombs, fast-moving clouds of steam and ash, and showers of particles that in a matter of days buried beneath 15 to 20 feet of ash nearly eight square miles of the valley floor, including the village whose remains we now call Ceren. By geological standards, that first and only eruption of Laguna Caldera was minor. To the families who hastily fled Ceren and the new volcano forming in the darkness less than a mile away, the event must have been terrifying. For Payson D. Sheets of the University of Colorado, the 1,400-year-old eruption provided a unique look—perhaps the best that any archaeologist will ever have—of the form and function of ancient Maya houses.

Structure 1, where a family ate, slept, made pottery and cotton thread, and stored food and implements—razor-sharp obsidian blades were clearly stashed out of reach of the children here—measured just over 155 square feet. It consisted of a single rectangular room fronted by a sheltered porch on the flat summit of a low, larger platform of fire-hardened clay mixed with grass. Its walls, anchored by sturdy corner columns, were made of the same tempered clay, packed smooth over vertical poles woven with horizontal sticks. They extended upward about five feet, enough for privacy. The frame of the pitched roof, elevated slightly to allow ventilation, was covered with thatch that, with the platform edge below, drained rainwater away from the living space.

In size, shape, and general plan, if not in material or details, the houses that Payson found at Ceren hardly differ from their counterparts built elsewhere in Mesoamerica from early Preclassic times to the present. Such dwellings not only filled the residential areas of the Maya cities but also formed the basis of ancient Maya architecture.

In the interests of politics and religion, and motivated by the absolute authority of their god-kings, the anonymous architects of the ancient Maya world took the two basic parts of the Maya dwelling place—the low platform and the roofed rectangle with a central doorway—and rendered them in astonishing, awesome, and seemingly infinite variety.

Consider the simple platform. Preclassic architects made it wider and higher, and in receding steps, until they reached the planned height and summit area. One or more stairways, built as the structure grew, completed the whole. The results of their skill endure—in the majestic structure that bulks over Lamanai in Belize, in the Lost World Pyramid of Preclassic Tikal, and in many others. In one form or another, and despite differences in style, the royal pyramid dominates most important Maya sites from Classic Copan to Postclassic Chichen Itza.

Status demanded that the basic Maya house be transformed into something more permanent as well, so the architects rendered it in stone or, in the unique case of Comalcalco in Tabasco, brick. In doing this they faced the difficult problem of the thatched roof and solved it with their famed corbel arch—an overhead converging vault made by overlapping flat stones toward the centerline of the room, braced for safety's sake during construction by wooden crossbeams. When there remained but a final slot of light, the masons covered it with capstones, then sealed the roof with plaster, making it convex for drainage.

The architect could stretch the basic rectangle, central-doorway combination at will, but always in the direction of the long axis, for the rooms could be no wider than their vaults permitted. This forced the architect to join rectangles in various ways to create structures of more than one room, or to interrupt existing rooms by adding walls. In rare cases—I am in awe of their defiance of gravity—a few architectural geniuses figured out how to make a vault turn a corner.

While the Maya architect often appears indifferent to the precision of right angles in the plans of platforms and buildings, he seldom violated the rule of bilateral symmetry: No matter what shape the layout formed in the end or how complicated it might be, its centerline must divide the whole—interior and exterior—into mirror images. By this rule, and depending on the size of the building, the single doorway might become three doorways, or five, or seven, or even nine—all odd numbers that force a central entrance. The physical exteriors of Maya buildings, naturally, reflect many of their inside construction features. The unusual height of inside vaults, for example, creates a correspondingly tall upper facade outside, the primary area for decoration.

In designing their buildings, the Maya not only drew on their skills as engineers but also paid homage to the cosmos itself. Each structure, no matter how intricate the masonry that held it together, was almost lovingly covered, inside and out, with a stucco coating that hid the stone joints. Often, key areas such as stairway flanks, building facades, roof combs—the tall stone superstructures that added height and grandeur to a building—and even interiors served as mediums for murals or carved and painted images of the gods and rulers. It's easy to forget, in contemplating a restored Maya temple or palace, that it also bore polychrome programs of political and religious art, much as does a modern billboard.

The buildings themselves also served as metaphors—pyramids as mountains, and temples as caves leading to the Underworld, their doorways made in the image of gaping monster mouths. In this manner, they formed suitable stages for the ritual pageants that reinforced the power of their kings. The first pyramid built at Cerros in northern Belize, around 50 B.C., provided just such a setting. As archaeologist David Freidel, who excavated it, and University of Texas art historian Linda Schele have shown, "from the foundation upward, the people made this building not only for, but with, devout and sacred action."

The small two-level platform faced south and was decorated with huge countenances of the sun and Venus arranged so that, to one facing the building, the central stairway divided the faces into east and west sets. On the east side, the lower mask is that of the rising sun, marked with the hieroglyph for first, or new. Above it stares Venus as morning star. On the opposite, or west, side of the platform, another stacked pair of celestial portraits represents the setting sun and Venus as evening star. The pattern forces the observer to behold, in effect, points on a vertical map of the sun as it circles through the Maya cosmos.

Such buildings were apparently considered to hold great power which, more often than not, they imparted to the spots they occupied. This appears to be the case at Copan, where Honduran archaeologist Ricardo Agurcia Fasquelle, a co-director of the Acropolis project, found a well-preserved Early Classic building, named Rosalila, beneath Structure 16, the highest temple on the Acropolis. According to Agurcia, Rosalila was accorded the reverence one normally associates with a human burial, with careful interment following the shrouding of its brightly painted stucco in a thick coat of plaster. To the Maya, buildings died just as did people, and apparently they were not soon forgotten: Sometime during the last period of the Maya occupation of Dzibilchaltun in Yucatan, a tunnel was opened to the Temple of the Seven Dolls, hidden deep in the heart of an even larger pyramid.

Maya architecture also took on meaning through vast systems of horizontal alignment. As Guatemalan archaeologist George F. Guillemin and Boston University art historian Clemency Chase Coggins have shown, Tikal's Great Plaza area was constructed in the form of a gigantic map, much like the two-level platform at Cerros. Here, though, the solar circuit lay on the ground. Temple I, the soaring funerary monument of the ruler Ah Cacao, occupies the east, or sunrise, position. Following an old Mesoamerican notion that equates north with up, the North Acropolis, at the zenith station, holds the mortuary pyramids of his revered predecessors, and sunset is manifest in Temple II, possibly a monument to Ah Cacao's wife. On the south side of the plaza, a long building with nine doorways, the number associated with the Maya Underworld, completes the cosmic circle.

Working with this holiest of places at the very center of Tikal, Vernon L. Scarborough of the University of Cincinnati has recently helped put the entire panorama of Maya architectural planning into balance. With meticulous surveys, he has confirmed a practical function of the city center: All its horizontal surfaces, from the plaster roofs of buildings to the Great Plaza itself, were subtly graded to convey precious rainfall to the city's reservoirs—a mundane but essential aspect of Maya architecture that recalls the primary function of the simple thatched roofs of the commoners of the city.

Using methods familiar to his ancestors, master mason Juan Chable sets guide strings for repositioning stones at Tulum, a Postclassic trade center on the coast of Quintana Roo.

FOLLOWING PAGES: Unique multistory tower caps the Palace at Palenque, whose mansard-style roofs and airy rooms characterize the city's public architecture.

122

*T*win towers of Rio Bec
Temple B in Campeche
mirror the style of architecture
found at Tikal and other Peten
sites. Though these 55-foot-high
solid towers provide beautiful
embellishment for the rooms
between them, they serve only for
show, with high temple doors that
lead nowhere and stairs that defy
climbing. Discovered in 1912, in
nearly intact condition, the Late
Classic palace soon disappeared,
swallowed by the forest, until its
rediscovery in 1973.

123

In Campeche, staring stone eyes top the monster-mouth doorway of a temple at Chicanna—which means "Serpent House" in Yucatec Mayan. Such doorways symbolized cave entrances, openings into the supernatural Underworld. Archaeologists found the temple in 1966, camouflaged by earth, roots, and trees (above). Excavation revealed a monument so well preserved that traces of red paint survived.

FOLLOWING PAGES: Called the finest portal arch in the Maya area, the Late Classic Labna Vault served as a ceremonial passageway between courtyards. El Mirador temple looms beyond. The lavish mosaic frieze on this side of the arch probably meant the more important courtyard was here; the eastern side was carved in simple geometric patterns. Two small rooms flank the arch.

Steep, narrow steps climb to the top of the Pyramid of the Magician at Uxmal. According to local lore, a dwarf took but a night to build the massive pyramid. To reach the Temple of the Magician at the summit — and a panoramic view of Uxmal and the surrounding forest — entails an arduous climb: This stairway rises at an angle of about 45 degrees; one on the opposite side climbs at 60 degrees. The Maya rebuilt and enlarged the temple-pyramid five times over the centuries. "So well built are they of cut stone in their fashion," wrote Bishop Diego de Landa of the Maya buildings, "that it fills one with astonishment."

129

*M*oonglow bathes the Caracol (above), a Terminal Classic building at Chichen Itza that may have served as an observatory for astronomical calculations. Puuc-style art decorates both the observatory and the platforms. Here in northern Yucatan, cultural ideas and architectural styles of the Maya blended with influences from central Mexico. At right, the sun rises behind columns representing Kukulcan—the Maya version of the Mexican deity Feathered Serpent—at the Toltec-style Temple of the Warriors. The reclining figure also reveals Toltec influence. The disk on his belly may have received the hearts of sacrificial victims as well as other offerings.

THE BUILDERS:

House of the Governor

"There is no rudeness or barbarity in the design or proportions; on the contrary, the whole wears an air of architectural symmetry and grandeur. . . ." Anyone who has stood in the early morning fog that often envelops the ruins of Uxmal can only agree with John Lloyd Stephens's first impression of the House of the Governor, the most imposing building at the site and, for many, the grandest single example of ancient American architecture.

The building, composed in three

RICHARD ALEXANDER COOKE III

parts connected by soaring transverse vaults, is 328 feet long and stands on the summit of an immense four-tiered platform that rises more than 50 feet above ground level. The entire complex was carefully placed to face the southernmost declination of Venus as morning star.

Art historian Jeff Karl Kowalski of Northern Illinois University, its principal modern investigator, believes it was built around A.D. 900 by the Uxmal ruler Lord Chac, and that the complex was both residence and administrative center. In only a century or so, it and the city it dominated were abandoned. Today the House of the Governor stands as the symbol of what Kowalski calls "a pivotal moment in the history of Maya architecture."

*C*opan's ball court lies near the foot of the Hieroglyphic Stairway. Such ritual courts were symbolic of the boundaries between the actual and supernatural worlds. Games were metaphors for the struggle between good and evil, and the ball echoed the trajectories of the heavenly bodies. On a vase (opposite), a costumed player lunges toward a rubber ball.

FOLLOWING PAGES: Flowers, symbols of divinity, blossom on banners at the San Juan Chamula Carnaval in Chiapas. The annual pre-Lenten festival goes on for five tumultuous days.

RELIGION AND RITUAL

by George E. Stuart

*I*nner doorway of Copan's Temple 22 rests on a row of weathered skulls and glyphs. Bacabs, or sky bearers, seated atop skulls that represent the Underworld, support a two-headed sky serpent. Bloodletting rituals held here by the ruler sustained the gods, who in turn granted humans bountiful harvests. Spiny oyster shells and stingray and sea urchin spines were used in such rituals. These, part of an offering buried beneath the altar that formed the base of

the Hieroglyphic Stairway, were placed there in dedication by Ruler Smoke Shell around A.D. 750. The shell contains red pigment and residue of incense burned during the ritual.

143

Gloved to protect fragile finds, archaeologists Robert Sharer and Loa Traxler remove a polychrome vase from a royal tomb excavated at Copan in the summer of 1992. Experts believe the chamber held the remains of a little-known king of the Copan dynasty. Other finds included jade and a necklace of carved shells. Although probably of local manufacture, some of the polychrome vessels (right) reflect a pottery style of Teotihuacan, the city in central Mexico whose influence spread across all of Early Classic Mesoamerica. Decorated with a layer of stucco and paint, two pots have human effigy lids. The three at center display sacred designs that were familiar across a vast geographical area; the other two bear glyphs in a Copan style.

Candles light the Underworld in Balankanche Cave near Chichen Itza, flickering before a natural formation that resembles the Maya's sacred World Tree. In a two-day ceremony, Maya and Catholic prayers and chants cleansed the cavern and, claimed the priest, brought rain. At a modern shrine near Chichicastenango, Guatemala, Maya priest Tomás Canil Marroquín ceremonially appeases an ancient deity, pouring sugarcane liquor onto its upturned stone lips. Such stone deities that are not given liquor periodically, the Maya believe, will cause people to perform violent acts.

FOLLOWING PAGES: Canil blesses a ritual fire and highland shrine with incense as his wife, Sebastiana Mejía Ventura, holds a rooster chosen for sacrifice. Many modern Maya, honoring ancestral beliefs, still dutifully worship the gods of nature and revere sacred landscapes.

Visually pleasing as well as informative, Maya writing used imagery as its base. Here the moon goddess holds a rabbit, an image the Maya saw—instead of a man—on the face of the moon. A lunar symbol curves to its right. Combined, the images represent "moon." An old scribe (opposite), with brush in hand and others bristling from his hat, reads bar-and-dot numbers aloud. FOLLOWING PAGES: A column of glyphs separates opposing images of Ruler 18 Rabbit at Copan. Such inscriptions recorded history and reinforced a king's divine right to his office.

BREAKING
THE CODE

by George E. Stuart

developed a series of maps of the lowlands with actual political boundaries—and, much like those in our modern world, these appear to have expanded or contracted through time, according to the fortunes of trade, warfare, and outside influences.

Through the efforts of Christopher Jones of the University Museum in Philadelphia, we can follow the career of Ah Cacao, "holy lord of the Tikal state," as he grows from the self-conscious celebrant at a calendar rite to full-fledged warrior-king 20 years later. Thanks to the work of Linda Schele and David Freidel, we can sense the impatience of Kan Xul II of Palenque as he bided his time until the death of his brother allowed him to be enthroned as "lord." Or we can consider their re-creation of the journey of Lady Six Sky, princess of Dos Pilas, as she moves along a Peten trail contemplating her imminent marriage to a noble of Naranjo.

Such reconstructions, though admittedly speculative, are valuable, for they serve to bring the ancient Maya to life in a plausible way. In the life of the princess, the appeal is heightened, for we know through the texts, as she did not know at the time, that her future son, Smoke Squirrel, one day would restore to greatness the Naranjo dynasty.

Lamentably, the Maya texts we have deciphered so far fail to speak of important things we wish very much to know firsthand—records of trade and commerce, inventories of building materials, listings of agricultural products. In short, what we have are almost exclusively the records of the elite. As one scholar put it, "Getting an idea of Maya society from such information is a little like trying to reconstruct the society of 19th-century England by analyzing the gravestones in Westminster Abbey."

In addition, the content of the existing hieroglyphic texts must be posed against other evidence if we are truly to know the ancient Maya. Given the source of the texts and the general propensity of any writing to be somewhat self-serving, we must be careful. "Not even the glyphs 'speak for themselves,'" cautions William A. Haviland of the University of Vermont, "and we need to check out what they say against the archaeological record."

David Stuart wrote, "For me, the ability to understand a text relies on precise phonetic transcription alongside reasonable caution in translating the meaning of ancient Maya terms. If such a standard is used, I would generously estimate that only about 50% of the Classic period inscriptions are literally 'readable.'"

The task ahead, I think epigraphists and archaeologists would agree, now lies in seeking a deeper perception of the world behind the glyphs. As many move toward that goal, the blank spots in the Maya hieroglyphic syllabary continue, sign by sign, to be filled.

Maya jigsaw puzzle: Archaeologists work to reassemble the massive Hieroglyphic Stairway, hundreds of its stones badly jumbled over the centuries.

*P*ancho, a spider-monkey
  resident of the ruins of
Copan, strolls past a small
pyramid. Gods in the form
of monkeys served as patrons of
scribes and artists, members
of professions revered by the
greatest lords. On one painted
bowl from Tikal, a holder of high
political office proudly boasted
that both of his parents were
scribes. The Maya believed their
supreme god, Itzamna, invented
writing, and apparently they kept
the sacred skill for a privileged
few, all from the elite class.
On a painted vase (detail below),
twin monkey gods work at
writing in a codex, or book.

163

Makeshift scaffold of lumber, limb, and rope makes a perch for David Stuart high atop the Corte, or cut, where the Copan River eroded part of the Acropolis over hundreds of years. David draws an inscription discovered in 1992 from an altar associated with one of the destroyed buildings. Maya writing alone cannot reveal all the secrets of their civilization. Aided by 19th-century photographs, written accounts of archaeological expeditions, fallen sculpture, and the Popol Vuh, artist Barbara Fash concluded that a now lost building with bat motifs here represented the mythical and horrible Bat House of the Maya Underworld. It may have imprisoned captives marked for sacrifice. Below, Barbara, David, and workmen Santos Rosa, left, and Francisco Canún reassemble blocks of text and sculpture from inside a temple that once topped the Hieroglyphic Stairway.

Scribed in many media and in various ways, Maya texts tell of the concerns of the elite. Part of a rare wooden lintel (left), dated 695, comes from Tikal ruler Ah Cacao's funerary monument and speaks of his mother, Lady Jaguar Throne. A glyph of painted stucco on a lock-top pot (above) uses syllables to spell out the vessel's use. The comb, ca, the fish, also ca, and the lower symbol, wa, spell ca-ca-wa, or cacao. The vessel held chocolate drink. On a stone lintel from Yaxchilan (opposite), a Long Count date uses glyphs of full figures as time periods and heads as numbers. The monkey at center right, symbol for a single day, holds the head for the number 6; the skull below it represents 10, for a total of 16. Multiplied by the one day, the glyph says "16 days." Combined, all the glyphs equal the date February 11, 526 B.C.

Graceful art of Classic Maya scribes survives in their calligraphy. Examples in the Cave of Naj Tunich (above) and in a tomb at Rio Azul (left), both in Guatemala, were executed 300 years apart. The 1,200-year-old Naj Tunich glyphs, painted in charcoal mixed with an oily base, remain undeciphered. Only eight years after its discovery in 1980, and after this photograph was taken, the fragile inscription was all but obliterated by vandalism. Done with a bold hand in Early Classic times, gods and symbols flank an inscription on the rear wall of the 1,500-year-old Rio Azul tomb, found in 1984. The glyph panel records the birth date of an unknown ruler as September 29, A.D. 417.

169

*S*telae rise in the plaza at Copan near a pyramid platform probably used in ceremonies marking the New Year. Always attuned to heavenly bodies and the passage of time, the Maya constructed buildings to observe and honor astronomical movements and important dates. An astronomer's keen eye (opposite) locks his gaze onto one of heaven's stars.

FOLLOWING PAGES: Rain-giving sky serpents writhe behind gods and rows of day glyphs in the Madrid Codex, which records dates appropriate for various ceremonies.

THE
CALENDAR

by George E. Stuart

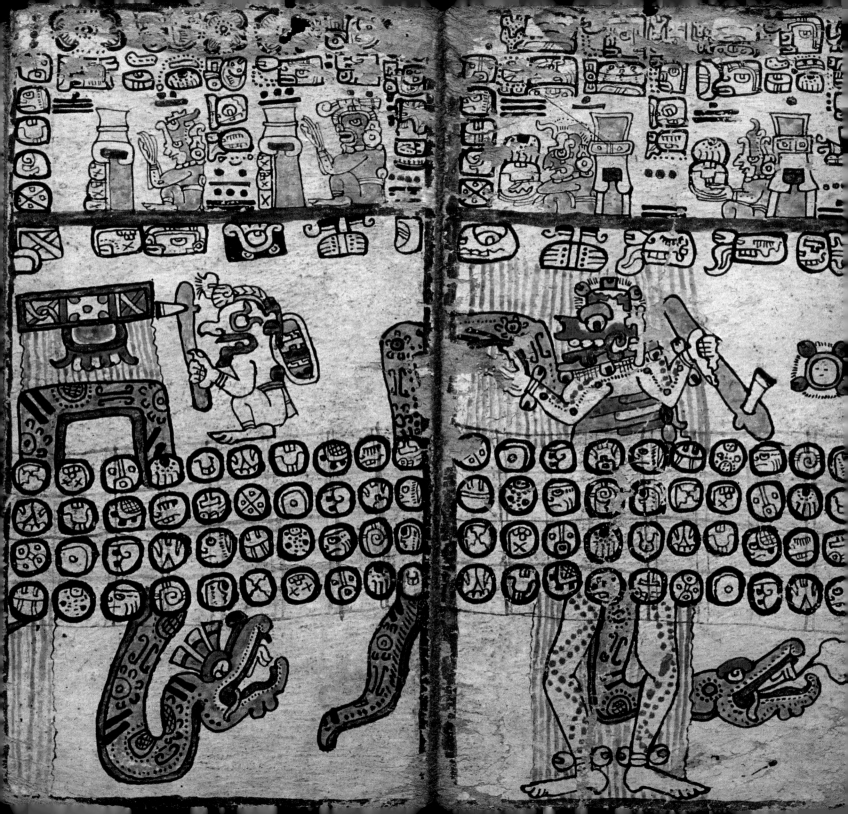

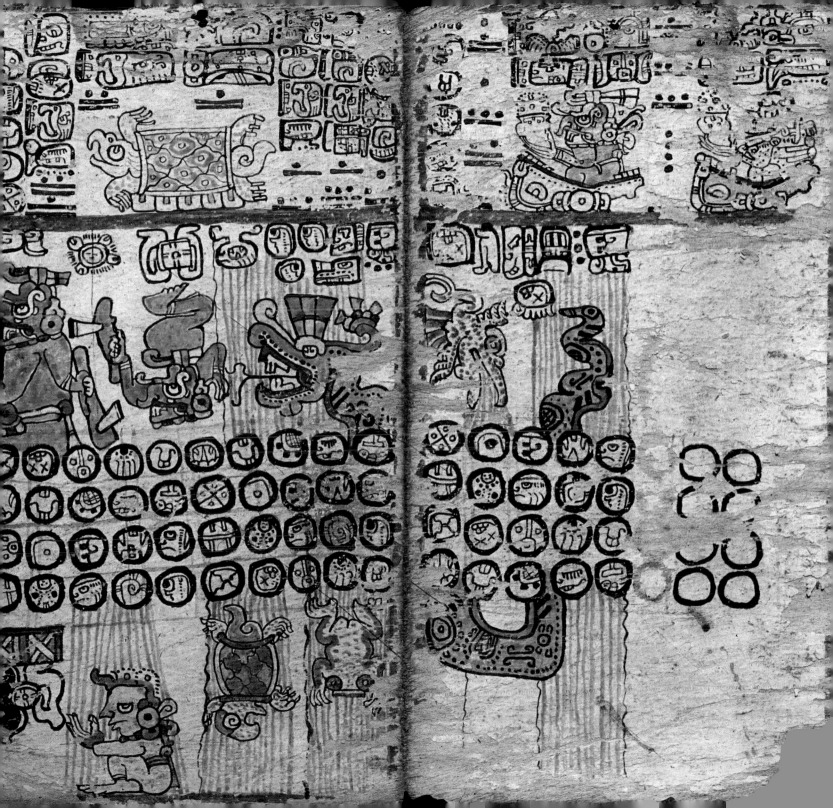

"**T**heir count is by fives up to twenty," reported Diego de Landa, referring to the Maya of Yucatan, "and by twenties up to one hundred and by hundreds up to four hundred, and by four hundreds up to eight thousand; and they used this method of counting very often in the cacao trading. They have other very long counts and they extend them *in infinitum*, counting the number 8000 twenty times, which makes 160,000; then again this 160,000 by twenty, and so on multiplying by 20, until they reach a number which cannot be counted."

Thus did Landa recognize a fundamental difference in the way the Maya counted things. He—and we—customarily use a numbering system based on counting fingers and reckoning in tens. The Maya, in contrast, used the whole person, both fingers and toes, and counted in twenties—a relationship reflected in the root shared by the Maya words *uinic,* which means "human being," and *uinal,* a calendar period of 20 days. The linkage of people and numbers is perhaps most evident in the system the Maya used to count the days of their lives. For them, the calendar was almost a living thing, an eternal procession of numbers and time periods moving as gods in mathematical precision through eternity.

The Maya calendar, an elaborated version of one inherited from their Preclassic Mesoamerican forebears, was based on the intermeshing of two main cycles—what we call the Sacred Round of 260 days and the Vague Year of 365 days. The Sacred Round is itself the product of two smaller cycles, the numbers 1 through 13, and 20 different day names. In contrast, the Vague Year is much like our solar year but without the fraction that forces us to use leap years—a correction the Maya ignored. Its 365-day span is divided into 18 months of 20 days each, plus a 5-day period at the end that the Maya considered a time of bad luck.

At some point after the invention of the Sacred Round and the Vague Year, a scheme was devised to link the two together into an even larger cycle. Because of the mathematics involved, the combination of the 260- and 365-day cycles results in a grander cycle of 18,980 days—about 52 solar years. Within this cycle, which Mayanists call the Calendar Round, each single day bears a twin label—its Sacred Round number and name, *and* its number and name in the Vague Year. For example, project the Maya calendar forward to January 20, 1993—Inauguration Day—and it falls on the Calendar Round date of 7 Akbal 6 Muan.

With its 52-year interval of repetition, the Calendar Round must have seemed, by itself, an inadequate measure for the endless chain of days. To overcome the problem, still another measure was incorporated into the system. We call it the Long Count. Brilliant in concept, yet relatively simple in its mechanism, this invention allowed the Classic Maya to tame eternity with an absolute chronology in which any given date was unique.

The Long Count employs the same base-20 arithmetic used to count cacao beans, but slightly modified for astronomical purposes. The Maya customarily expressed it as a string of five numbers, including zeros when necessary, paired with hieroglyphs for time periods—the 144,000-day *baktun*, the 7,200-day *katun*, the 360-day *tun*, the 20-day *uinal*, and the *kin*, or single day. With their numerical coefficients, these form a series of products whose sum equals the number of days that had elapsed since the creation of the world, a date deep in mythical time that, according to the calendar correlation we now use, equals August 13, 3114 B.C.

The Maya calendar scribes set this day of creation at 4 Ahau in terms of the Sacred Round and 8 Cumku of the Vague Year, then constructed a Long Count notation especially for it: They expanded the usual five places of the normal version—13.0.0.0.0—to a full 24 places, creating a monstrous number that literally locked that profoundly important day in the context of eternity.

I'll not forget the day I first saw Stela 1 at the ruins of Coba, for the expanded Long Count date of Maya creation appears there in its rare complete form. Although the period glyphs have been all but obliterated by the onslaught of the 1,300 rainy seasons that have come and gone since the stone was raised, the hierarchy of numbers appears in all its glory when the sunlight hits it right. The resulting number almost defies translation, for it would take more than 40 *octillion* years—that is, 40 followed by 27 zeros—merely for it to come around again. The interval is approximately equal to the 15-billion-year span that separates us from the cosmic "big bang" multiplied almost 3,000,000,000,000,000,000 times! In confronting cycles of such awesome magnitude, I felt I had caught a glimpse of infinity.

It must have seemed almost child's play for the mathematicians, when Pacal, ruler of Palenque, ordered that the 80th Calendar Round anniversary of his accession—July 29, 615, in our terms—be calculated into the future. The date, as determined by Mayanists Linda Schele and David Freidel from a carved tablet in the Temple of the Inscriptions, would be October 23, 4772.

Beginning with the "zero date" of creation, in its five-place form, the Long Count functioned for the Maya, as for us, as a kind of majestic odometer of time, clicking off the days in lockstep with the Calendar Round and providing a precise cadence to which the astronomers matched the movements of the visible planets, the constellations, and the recurring visits of heavenly gods and ancestors.

For me, the intimate relationship between Maya calendar and Maya culture takes its most tangible form in what Christopher Jones defined as the "twin pyramid groups" at Tikal. There are nine of these and, like the layout of the Great Plaza, they constitute an example of what Chris's colleague, archaeologist Wendy Ashmore, calls "maps of the proper structure of the cosmos"—special buildings placed on the axes of the cardinal directions to serve as stages for public ritual. Early in his investigations at Tikal, Chris Jones tabulated the Long Count dates recorded in each of the site's twin pyramid groups. These contained a pattern of numbers showing that all were built and dedicated at the end of a katun, the 20-year period that stands in the fourth position of the Long Count date. For the Maya, the katun was a very special period. Its interval—7,200 days, or almost 20 solar years—made it the largest station within the Long Count likely to occur at least one time, perhaps more, in any lifetime or reign. Whatever the attraction of the katun, it appears to have marked the significant divisions of Maya history and ritual for more than a thousand years.

Clues to one such katun ritual may be seen on two monuments discovered in the rubble of a twin pyramid group razed in ancient times for a renovation of Tikal. Altar 14 contains the Long Count date 9.13.0.0.0 and the Calendar Round date on which it fell, 8 Ahau 8 Uo, along with the name of the current ruler, Ah Cacao. The gigantic 8 Ahau glyph, centering the top of the altar, leaves no doubt about its purpose: It is the name of the katun. The celebrant, Ah Cacao himself, appears on the accompanying Stela 30 in full ritual regalia.

The ceremony for Katun 8 Ahau that took place on March 18, 692, must have been a sight to behold, a splendid pageant accompanied by the moaning intonations of conch-shell trumpets and wooden horns against the staccato click of rattles and bone rasps and the deep cadence of wooden and clay drums. The ruler, richly garbed in a kilt of white cotton secured by a heavy belt hung with jade plaques and shells, wore a massive collar of jade beads the size of golf balls—he would later be buried with these. Tall by Maya standards, Ah Cacao's appearance was enhanced by an elaborate headdress made of the brightly painted and jawless wooden mask of a god decorated with ornaments and iridescent green quetzal plumes. He carried a wooden staff ornamented with seashells and intricate carvings of the faces of the gods of rulership.

While thousands watched from the plaza, the celebrants, including members of Tikal's highest ranking families, moved from station to station amid clouds of aromatic resin incense, pausing at each for the prescribed chants and recitations. At high noon, the culmination of the ritual, Ah Cacao, alone, entered the stone enclosure on the north side of the plaza, leaned his staff against the wall, and with appropriate solemnity, drew blood from his penis with an obsidian lancet. That act of bloodletting reaffirmed, for the whole of the katun to come, the link between Ah Cacao and the sacred calendar that regulated the lives of his people.

The use of the Long Count died in A.D. 909, one of the casualties of the Classic Period collapse, but the katun survived well into the Colonial Period as the main framework for the recording of Maya history and prophecy. Even Landa managed to muster a grudging admiration for the last vestige of the ancient calendar: "If it was the Devil who devised this count of *Katuns*, then he did so, as he is accustomed, for his own honor; and, if it was a man, he must have been a fine idolator because . . . he devised all the principal deceits, divinations and delusions under which these people labored. . . ."

Praying to the earth, day-keeper Andrés Xiloj of Momostenango, Guatemala, begins a divination using seeds and the 260-day Maya calendar to determine auspicious dates.

BOB SACHA

180

*F*rom the central doorway in Uxmal's House of the Governor, John Carlson, an archaeoastronomer, sights along an ancient line. Unlike the roughly north-south orientation of most of the city, this royal palace faces southeast. About A.D. 900, when the building was completed, a Maya standing in this spot would have looked across the top of a pyramid three miles distant to the place on the horizon where Venus rose as the morning star at its southernmost declination. Because Uxmal and other Puuc cities depended solely on rainy-season water stored in cisterns, all honored the rain god Chac, and Uxmal's ruler at the time the palace was built took the deity's name. More than 200 stone mosaic masks of Chac appear on the palace facade. In deference to the planet, their lower eyelids all bear the symbol for Venus.

Sunsets at the spring and autumn equinoxes bring crowds to the Castillo at Chichen Itza (below) to witness a serpentine body of light and shadow slither down the stairway on the left to a stone serpent head at the bottom. Some believe the Maya oriented the building, also known as the Temple of Kukulcan, or Feathered Serpent, for this singular appearance of the god. Many Maya buildings stood as symbols uniting the cosmos. At Tikal (opposite), Venus and Jupiter align above Temple I. To the Maya, such pyramids symbolized earth's sacred mountains.

Powerfully human visage of the sun god, some six feet tall and carved in stucco over a stone base, flanks a pyramid stairway at Kohunlich in Quintana Roo. Such masks decorated many Late Preclassic and Early Classic temples as rulers sought to associate themselves with the gods. T-shaped tooth and barbels protruding from the corners of his mouth identify this god as the sun. At right, a leering old man forces his dubious charms on a young woman in a Late Classic clay figurine from Jaina. They probably portray the sun and the moon, wedded deities in many Maya traditions.

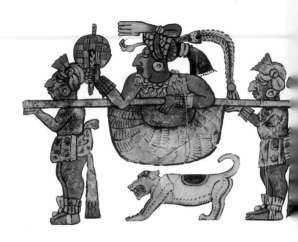

Postclassic port of call on the Yucatan Peninsula sea-trade route, Tulum specialized in the export of honey. Wealthy merchants, like the trader shown here, may have governed the city.

FOLLOWING PAGES: Putting head, neck, and back to the task, a modern-day vendor in Santiago Atitlan, Guatemala, uses a tumpline to distribute the weight of a heavy and cumbersome load.

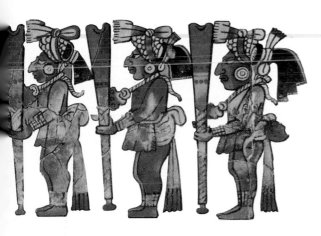

THE MERCHANTS

by Gene S. Stuart

served as the principal currency, units of international commercial exchange.

When canoes departed from Xicalango, most hugged the shore, using natural landmarks, shrines, lookout towers, and signal fires as navigational aids. Settlements and natural harbors dotted the shoreline. Rulers of inland cities often controlled commercial ports, and Chichen Itza had Isla Cerritos just off the coast. Mexican archaeologist Tomás Gallareta of INAH and Anthony P. Andrews of the New College of the University of South Florida excavated there, finding "ruins of docks and piers, while on its south shore a sea wall more than 1,000 feet long encloses an artificial harbor that once offered refuge to large numbers of canoes."

Rounding the northeastern tip of the peninsula, the traders entered the turquoise waters of the Caribbean and put into busy east coast ports, some of which also served as pilgrimage sites. Cozumel Island had a shrine to Ix Chel, the moon goddess. Down the coast, the bright blue buildings of Tulum sat high on a cliff above a sandy beach. Farther south, the large town of Chetumal controlled an intersection of sea trade and overland commerce. In the southern extreme of the Gulf of Honduras the Chontal Maya traders reached their eastern destination: the busy ports of Nito and Naco.

A canoe making the journey from Xicalango to Naco covered a distance of about a thousand miles. At Nito and Naco the Putun exchanged goods with traders from far south of the Maya realm who had also made incredible journeys, some traveling from as far away as Panama and Costa Rica.

Postclassic Maya ruling families were not above taking an active role in the trade and commerce they controlled. When Mayapan fell to the rival Xiu family, the ruler and all his sons but one were killed. The merchant prince who escaped death was away in Honduras on a business trip.

Columbus, on his fourth and final voyage to the New World in 1502, encountered a trading canoe near the Bay Islands in the Gulf of Honduras. This was probably his only meeting with natives of the mainland. Eyewitnesses and chroniclers recorded that more than 25 men, as well as women and children, traveled in a craft eight feet wide and as long as a Spanish galley, with a cabin amidships. Bartolomé de las Casas, the Bishop of Chiapas, listed a cargo that included cotton mantles, huipils, and loincloths, all with multicolored designs; wooden swords fitted with sharp flint blades, copper bells and axes, and large quantities of cacao beans. Eric Thompson believed these voyagers may have set out from Xicalango, stopping at many ports to deal in goods from many regions. He wrote: "One may guess that merchants and crew were Putun . . . the Phoenicians of Middle America."

An explosion of color—plastic housewares, as well as decorative fruits and vegetables—dazzles the eye at a market display in Merida, Yucatan.

*M*arket day, a traditional
weekly event throughout
Guatemala, unleashes a flood of
sights, sounds, and smells as
vendors spread their wares—
from onions and cauliflowers
to chili peppers, radishes,
squashes, and potatoes. In
Chichicastenango, a woman
offers chickens; a youngster in
Zunil finds a moment of respite
atop a sack of corn.

Ek Chuah, Pinocchio-nosed god of the Maya merchants, cavorts on a painted vase. In his right hand he holds a fan, symbol of merchants. At night, according to Bishop Landa, travelers "offered prayers to . . . Ek Chuah, that he would bring them back home again in safety." Recently unearthed at Cacaxtla, some 80 miles east of Mexico City, a Classic Maya-style mural

(opposite) decorates a stairway. It portrays an itinerant trader, perhaps pausing to catch his breath after propping his pack on his lance, which doubled as a walking stick. His wide-brimmed, monster-topped hat is attached to a backpack laden with salt, quetzal feathers, and a turtle shell from the distant Gulf coast. Cacaxtla was a major commercial crossroads at its height between 650 and 900. Trails converging there bore processions of armed warrior merchants weighted

down with exports—obsidian, textiles, and pumice for grinding corn. They returned carrying cacao, quetzal feathers, and prisoners destined for sacrifice.

JUSTIN KERR; ENRICO FERORELLI (OPPOSITE)

Luxury goods—plumes of the scarlet macaw, cacao, and tail feathers of the legendary quetzal (opposite)—ranked among the items prized by the Maya. From cacao came chocolate, a drink of the upper classes; the bean itself also was used as money and was harvested from plantations controlled by nobles. Bird feathers made distinctive adornments. Only the ruling class wore the quetzal's long, sweeping tail feathers, plucked from live birds.

According to one chronicler, any commoner who killed a quetzal faced certain death. These and other goods—salt, textiles, animal pelts, honey, grinding stones, copper ornaments, and ceramics—often were carried by Chontal Maya traders. During the Postclassic Period their giant canoes monopolized the sea routes around the Yucatan Peninsula between present-day Laguna de Terminos and Honduras. A single large canoe could carry far more cargo—faster and more cheaply—than a host of overland traders.

A Maya boatbuilder gives shape and grace to a dugout canoe along the banks of the Dulce River in Guatemala. In ancient times, craftsmen laboriously carved both large and small vessels into shape with stone or shell adzes. To hollow out the craft, they lit fires along the log and scraped away the charred wood. In Chiapas (below), boaters from Corozal pole down the Usumacinta River. This mode of travel, common since early Maya times, still serves today.

THE MERCHANTS:
Luxury Goods

When the Aztec emperor Moctezuma II heard of Hernán Cortés's arrival on the Gulf shores of Veracruz in 1519, he suspected the visitor might be divine and sent gifts fit for a god. His emissaries dressed Cortés in the treasured trappings of the god Quetzalcoatl, the Feathered Serpent— "the turquoise mosaic snake mask with the head fan of quetzal feathers," according to Franciscan friar Bernardino de Sahagún. And then, "on his arm they laid the shield with bands of gold and shells crisscrossed and with outspread quetzal feathers. . . ." The Spanish leader coolly asked, "Are these all your gifts of greeting, all your gifts for coming. . . ?" He had found that the Old and New Worlds placed the highest commercial value on different commodities. Spaniards sought gold, and Cortés did not know—or was too arrogant to acknowledge—that quetzal plumes were so precious to Aztecs and Maya that they adorned only royalty and gods. Quetzals lived chiefly in the mountain forests. Trappers captured the birds at watering places, took tail feathers, and set the birds free. Trapping rights were inherited and guaranteed great wealth. According to Bartolomé de las Casas, the Bishop of Chiapas, to capture or kill a

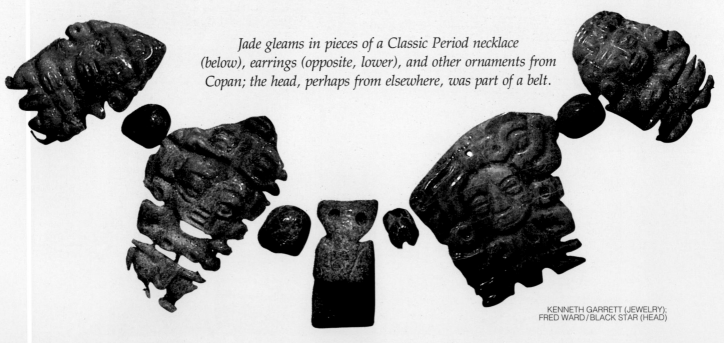

Jade gleams in pieces of a Classic Period necklace (below), earrings (opposite, lower), and other ornaments from Copan; the head, perhaps from elsewhere, was part of a belt.

KENNETH GARRETT (JEWELRY);
FRED WARD / BLACK STAR (HEAD)

seized the metal. Said Sahagún, quoting local sources, "clearly their thirst for gold was insatiable; they starved for it; they lusted for it; they wanted to stuff themselves with it as if they were pigs." The Maya never placed the highest value on gold, but, possibly because of its amazing color and because of their love of metaphors, the Yucatec Maya called it *takin*—excrement of the sun. The word endures today as a kind of metaphor for trade, for in modern Yucatec, takin

quetzal in Alta Verapaz was a capital offense, for "these feathers were things of great value because they used them as money." Apart from their beauty, the brilliant green of quetzal plumes made them sacred. They resembled the color of corn leaves, the plant of life. And so did the color of jade. Traders obtained precious jade mainly from the Motagua River Valley in the Guatemalan highlands. The jade trade was lucrative and sometimes proved a two-way street: After exporting the raw material to the lowlands, highlanders imported it back again in the form of figurines and ornaments carved by more expert lowland artisans. For the Maya, metal became important only in the Postclassic Period. The greatest number of metal objects yet found in the Maya area came from the Cenote of Sacrifice at Chichen Itza. Finds included a gold cup and saucer, and gold and copper jewelry and disks embossed with battle scenes. As Cortés approached the Aztec capital of Tenochtitlan, Spanish reaction to the gifts that included gold amazed the Aztecs. The Spaniards greedily

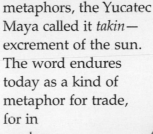

means "money." And Guatemalans still honor one of the most treasured resources of their past: Their official unit of currency is called the quetzal.

CONQUEST

*Old and new stand shoulder to shoulder in Acanceh, Yucatan,
where Coca-Cola and an Early Classic pyramid share a dusty street
with Maya women wearing traditional huipils.*

Christianity triumphant: The Monastery of San Antonio in Izamal was begun in 1553—on an ancient Maya platform, with Maya workmen using stones from Maya temples. In the huge atrium, throngs of newly converted Indians gathered to be baptized, catechized, and preached to. At a dance in Guatemala (opposite) a youngster doffs his conquistador mask.

FOLLOWING PAGES: In Chichicastenango, masked revelers perform the Dance of the Party Guests, mimicking Colonial Spaniards and their festive costumes of the court.

A LONG SURRENDER

by Gene S. Stuart

The first known mainland encounter between Spaniards and Maya occurred when a Spanish caravel sank near Jamaica in 1511. According to Bishop Landa, "not more than twenty men escaped. These, together with Valdivia [an official], took to the small boat without sails and with poor oars and without any food. They wandered over the sea for thirteen days. After nearly half had perished from hunger, they reached the shore of Yucatan at a province which was called Maya. . . ."

They washed onto an eastern province whose ruler made a sacrifice and feast of Valdivia and four others. But the king found Gonzalo Guerrero, Gerónimo de Aguilar, and their surviving companions too thin to eat. Said Aguilar, "I, together with six others, remained in a coop, in order that for another festival that was approaching, being fatter, we might solemnize their banquet with our flesh."

The desperate Spaniards escaped to a rival and "more merciful" lord who "made use of them as his slaves," but all perished of disease except Aguilar and Guerrero. They survived a pestilence—possibly smallpox—that struck the peninsula in 1515 or 1516, the first of the Old World diseases, including measles, influenza, and typhus, that decimated the population.

Soon Spanish explorers were skirting peninsular shores in annual forays. In 1517, Francisco Hernández de Córdoba sailed from Havana on a voyage of discovery and trade. Dazzled by fantasies of riches, Juan de Grijalva set out in 1518 along with Pedro de Alvarado, who would later subdue the highland Maya in Guatemala, and Francisco de Montejo, who would conquer the peninsula. On the east coast, Grijalva's chaplain reported "a city or town so large, that Seville would not have seemed more considerable nor better; one saw there a very large tower. . . ." It was probably Tulum. In the Gulf of Mexico, Grijalva explored near Xicalango, the great Maya port, and touched the edge of the Aztec empire in Veracruz.

The next year brought Hernán Cortés, with Captains Montejo and Alvarado. The expedition first landed on Cozumel Island, where they destroyed idols and erected a cross. Hearing news of "bearded men," they contacted Aguilar, who "cried with delight" and gladly joined Cortés, who then sailed on to conquer the Aztecs. Guerrero, though, had made his way south to Chetumal, become war chief to the lord Nachan Can, married a royal lady, and had great "love for his children." Aguilar said that Guerrero declined an offer of rescue in part because he had "his nostrils, lips, and ears pierced and his face painted and his hands tattooed. . . ." Guerrero had happily become Maya, and a man of high rank at that. Later Spaniards met their military match because of him: He had trained his Maya soldiers in Spanish battle tactics.

After gaining a reputation for shocking cruelty in the Aztec conquest, Alvarado, under orders from Cortés, swept southward into the fragmented Maya kingdoms of the highlands. On December 6, 1523, he left Mexico City with 300 infantry, 120 cavalry, and a small force of Mexican Indians. He was a heartless but handsome man. A soldier who served with him wrote: "He was about thirty-four years old when he came here, of good size, and well proportioned, with a very cheerful countenance and a winning smile, and because he was so handsome the Mexican Indians gave him the name of 'Tonatio,' which means 'the Sun.'"

From the outset, the Spanish shrewdly played rival group against group to facilitate conquest, and because of animosity between the leading highland Maya—the Cakchiquel and the Quiche—the powerful Cakchiquel joined in the final defeat of their Quiche enemies in 1524. A decisive battle had taken place in a valley where Spanish and Quiche armies clashed hand to hand. Alvarado reported: "We commenced to crush them and scattered them in all directions and . . . made the greatest destruction in the world, at a river." Tecum, Quiche military leader and grandson of the king, struck down Alvarado's horse before himself falling. He was wearing quetzal feathers on his arms and legs, mirrors on his chest, forehead, and back, and a crown of gold and precious stones. According to legend, the valley came to be called Quezaltenango—"place of the quetzal"—for the plumes he wore. The river name translates as "blood river" for the color it ran by battle's end.

A Guatemalan legend says that about 30,000 Quiche died that day, and after the battle a great multitude of quetzals descended from the sky and came to rest on the slain warriors, covering them with their outstretched wings. When they rose again, their breasts were soaked in blood; to this day the males wear bright crimson breast feathers in memory of the fallen heroes.

Alvarado established the first colonial capital of Guatemala on July 25, 1524, at Iximche, the Cakchiquel capital. His conquest proved profitable: Indians provided gold as tribute, and the Pacific slopes grew cacao of such superb flavor it was reserved for the Spanish. But it was an uneasy alliance, and the Cakchiquel soon staged an unsuccessful revolt, establishing a pattern of Maya resistance that would continue for centuries.

After the defeat of the Quiche, Cortés set out from Mexico City for Honduras to quell the rebellion of a Spanish official. He was the first European to journey through the wilderness of the southern Maya lowlands. In March 1525 his army reached Lake Peten Itza, and the king, Canek, showed the Spanish leader his island capital, Tayasal. Cortés pushed on through treacherous terrain, but left in their charge "a horse whose foot was pierced by a stick and who was unable to walk. . . . The lord promised me that he would cure it." Unfamiliar with horses, the Itza worshiped the beast as a god. They offered it chicken and other meat as food and presented it with ritual offerings of flowers. When the creature soon died the Itza carved an image of their new god in stone, but seated as if it had been a deity in human form.

Cortés and Alvarado became wealthy from their exploits in the New World. And in 1527, Francisco de Montejo sought to increase his fortune in the conquest of Yucatan. But, though he had an army eager for quick victory and valuable plunder, the endeavor was to drag on for 19 miserable years.

Historian Robert S. Chamberlain wrote of an early foray: "The way was rough, the sun was hot, and almost the whole route lay through heavy bush, ideal for ambuscades." Within six months, disease and warfare had reportedly reduced Montejo's force of some 275 men to about 75. Chamberlain concluded, "Few New World expeditions suffered so severely within such a brief period."

As the years passed, some Maya swore loyalty; others, reported Montejo, proved "bellicose, valiant, and experienced in war. . . ." Spanish reinforcements were light and desertions heavy. After seven years, a despondent Montejo wrote to his king, "There is not a single river, although there are lakes, and the hills are of live rock, dry and waterless. . . . No gold has been discovered, nor is there anything from which advantage can be gained." He held his army together with threats and promises, while, wrote Landa, "the Indians, thinking that it was a harsh thing to serve foreigners in lands where they were themselves lords, began to attack him on all sides." Spanish victories came slowly. The eastern provinces rebelled in November 1546, when enraged Maya rose up and killed or sacrificed some 20 Spaniards, their families, their Maya servants, and everything "that savoured of the Spanish, including the herds. . . ." The revolt was subdued by March 1547 and marked the official completion of the conquest of Yucatan.

In theory, the only Maya still independent were the Itza, isolated in the wilderness of central Peten in Guatemala. Then, in 1618, Franciscan priests Bartolomé de Fuensalida and Juan de Orbita visited Tayasal, determined to Christianize still another king called Canek, and his people. The ruler declined, saying, "the time had not yet arrived in which their ancient Priests had prophesied to them they were to relinquish the worship of their Gods. . . ." Seeing the image of the horse god—by then nearly a century old—an infuriated Father Orbita smashed it to bits, which outraged the Itza. Reaching the end of their patience as official Christian missions continued, the Itza in 1623 slaughtered a priest, several Spanish soldiers, and some 90 Christian Maya during a Mass.

An amazing new discovery reveals a secret and previously unknown mission by a Franciscan friar that took place probably early in 1695.

In 1988, while in Mexico, George obtained four pages of a manuscript whose words were so faded they had become virtually invisible. Alfred M. Yee, of National Geographic's Photographic Services, photographed the sheets under ultraviolet light, and the lost words reappeared. The document has since been presented by the Society to the government of Mexico. In translating the recovered words, ethnohistorian Grant D. Jones of Davidson College found that they recorded a visit to the Itza and, astonishingly, vividly described the last king of the Maya.

According to the account, perhaps from an educated Yucatec Maya, Fray Andrés de Avendaño y Loyola and his companions spent a fearful night in a town on Lake Peten Itza. In the morning they heard a great cry from the local Indians. "And looking up we saw that there came from the direction of the rising sun a great wedge of canoes, all of them adorned with many flowers and playing much music with sticks and with drums and wooden flutes. And seated in one larger than all was the king of the Itzas, who is the Lord Canek, which means the star twenty serpent. . . . King Canek had himself very well adorned, on his golden head a large crown of pure gold with a crest of gold, and he wore his ears covered with gold disks. And the disks have hangings that shake and fall over the shoulders like tatters, and likewise on his arms he wears rings of pure gold. And on the fingers of his hands he also wears rings of gold. And he dresses in a tunic, pure white in color, that is completely adorned with embroideries of the color blue. . . . And he girds his waist with a broad sash like a fastening, but this is black and means that Canek is also priest of the Itzas. And his sandals are . . . made of blue thread with many gold jingles. . . . When Canek arrived at the shore of the lake, they put down a long mat so that he could walk on it."

The king took the party to Tayasal, fed and housed them, and "Lord Canek said that whenever we might come on another occasion he would give us the answer as to whether his family and he might cleave and receive the Holy Sacrament of baptism. . . ." But too many Caneks had delayed too long. On March 13, 1697, a Spanish military force overthrew Tayasal in a single morning.

The conquest of the Maya had taken 173 years.

During the Colonial Period, Spaniards wisely allowed the surviving Maya nobility to continue to administer—under their command. But populations dropped alarmingly. Warfare, famine, and epidemics swept Mesoamerica. In Yucatan alone, between 1639 and 1736, the native population declined 40 percent from an already seriously depleted population. Many families fled to areas beyond Spanish control. Vast haciendas held many Maya in a system of lifelong debt peonage, falsifying accounts, paying low wages, and punishing delinquents at the whipping post. The state levied impossible taxes and sold orphans as servants, even if they had close relatives to support them.

Both highland and lowland Maya rebelled, and whites retaliated. In 1761 a *batab,* or local chief, of Cisteil in Yucatan gathered 1,500 followers and crowned himself King Canek. Infuriated whites killed 500 Maya and marched Canek to Merida, where he was drawn and quartered. The most famous Maya rebellion came with Yucatan's War of the Castes. The war lasted from 1847 to 1855; the overall revolt until 1902, when Mexico created the territory of Quintana Roo from restless eastern provinces. But the spirit of strife endured long afterward.

During the 1970s, our family lived for several months in the ancient ruins of Coba in Quintana Roo. A village of hardworking farmers had sprung up in that rain forest frontier, a place of new beginnings that reflected old Maya values and traditional beliefs. But once, in quiet conversation, some elderly villagers spoke of dreadful times past and bitter memories from an age they will not forget. One man, respected for his dignity and leadership, claimed that as a boy during the unrest that followed the War of the Castes he had drunk the blood and feasted on the brains of a white man.

Dios Cristo y hombre
Vive Reina y ympera
1901

216

*A*zure-clad saints, angels, and cherubs welcome churchgoers to a service in the highland Guatemala town of San Andres Xecul. Once converted to Christianity, the Maya found parts of their new religion compatible with some of their old beliefs. Maya deities became Christian saints, and churchly rituals were largely interchangeable. Thus, Ix Chel, a moon goddess, was worshiped as the Virgin Mary, and the churchyard, carefully oriented to the cardinal directions, became the focus of ceremonial activities.

FOLLOWING PAGES: Shouldering a float during Good Friday observances near Antigua Guatemala, worshipers dressed in purple— symbol of Christ's Passion—reenact His journey to Calvary. The inscription reads, "Jesus and His Disciples at the Last Supper." Easter celebrations last a week in Guatemala, and processions occur daily. Each church has its special saint, whose statues are carried by celebrants.

217

GUILLERMO ALDANA E.; KENNETH GARRETT (RIGHT)

uarding a balcony at Casa Montejo in Merida, Spanish halberdiers stand atop the heads of vanquished Indians (opposite). The artist copied this method of showing triumph over enemies from Maya art. Francisco de Montejo, conqueror of Yucatan, built the house. A young worker (below) boots a flatcar of henequen fiber out of a mill built in 1912. Leaves are shredded to separate pulp from fiber, which is then sun dried and twisted into cordage. The industry peaked in Yucatan in the late 19th century, providing rigging for sailing ships.

A LONG SURRENDER:
War of the Castes

In the early days of 1847, Maya diviners in Yucatan read their calendar using grains of sacred corn and discovered an awesome portent—dangerous times were approaching.

At that time, some 140,000 people of Spanish descent and mestizos—whom the Maya considered to be white as well—lived in Yucatan. Although at least 75 percent of the population was Maya, whites administered three of the four regions from the aristocratic centers of Merida, Campeche, and Valladolid. The fourth region of independent Indian villages with traditional chiefly leadership lay to the south and east—the little-known frontier. Beyond stretched the uncharted and mysterious rain forest.

In the spring of 1847, Maya farmers planted their corn as usual, and the rains came as hoped, but frontier chiefs had secretly amassed supplies and sent surreptitious messages. An alarmed hacienda owner reported seeing Indians on the move, and a Maya chief was executed. Small-scale Indian attacks began.

Then, on July 30, after 300 years of virtual enslavement, a violent uprising exploded. Several white families fell to Maya rebels who massacred men, women, and children alike. On August 6, all white men from 16 to 60 were drafted for military duty. As the Maya looted and burned haciendas and towns and bought arms from British Honduras—now Belize—fighting increased, and both sides reported unspeakable atrocities. Even infants were not excused the color of their skin.

By January 1848 an estimated 12,000 to 15,000 Maya held Valladolid under siege. In March many refugees managed to flee the city through a breach soldiers blasted in the barricades. Historian Nelson Reed wrote: "The congested and tormented column was attacked along its entire length, with skirmishing where there were soldiers, slaughter where there were none. For the Maya, it was a grand orgy of revenge, their enemy too scattered for effective defense, and the machete quite sufficient for the unarmed."

By late May, when the dry season drew to an end and oppressive daily temperatures soared into the hundreds, Maya armies held most of the peninsula. One force of rebels had pushed to the suburbs of Campeche; others were advancing on Merida. Refugees had increased that city's population of 48,000 to an encampment of 100,000.

Desperate, the military planned a fighting withdrawal toward the tiny port of Sisal, where ships of several nations waited to take on evacuees, but there was not enough paper left to print the order. News spread by rumor in Campeche and Merida: The Maya intended a general slaughter. Braced for the final attack, the cities waited in terror throughout a day and a night, then another. The military sent out scouts: The Maya armies had vanished. Years later, Leandro Poot, son of one of the Maya leaders, explained what had happened: Winged ants, harbingers of the first rain, had begun to swarm. The Maya said, "The time has come for us to make our planting, for if we do not we shall have no Grace of God to fill the bellies of our children." And then, "in spite of the supplications and threats of the chiefs, each man rolled up his blanket and put it in his food pouch, tightened the thongs of his sandals, and started for his home and his cornfield."

An anonymous artist captures the 19th-century fighting between the Yucatec Maya and the Spanish.

TODAY

Fetching water, a child fills a jar in Chichicastenango, Guatemala. Today more than four million Maya make up the largest native American group north of Peru.

Lost in thought, a man in San Jorge, Guatemala, is oblivious to a boy's play nearby. Once the people of great kingdoms, most Maya today belong to the poorest classes of Mesoamerica. At a 1987 festival of native cultures in Jocotan, Guatemala, a celebrant (opposite) munches an age-old treat, freshly cooked corn on the cob.

FOLLOWING PAGES: Mist veils Easter services in Chamula in Chiapas. Worshipers enhance the sacredness of Christian crosses with pine—a symbol of life.

DAVID ALLEN HARVEY (BELOW AND FOLLOWING PAGES); RICHARD ALEXANDER COOKE III (OPPOSITE); GIANNI VECCHIATO (PRECEDING PAGES)

THE LIVING MAYA

by Gene S. Stuart

Just as their ancestors took great delight in language and reveled in puns and poetic turns of phrase, the Maya of today enjoy describing their world in metaphor. Eric Thompson recorded modern wordplay in the Yucatan Peninsula: "A girl or a boy approaching marriage age is called 'maize plant coming into flower'; a meddler is rebuked with the words, 'Why are you wearing a loincloth that is not yours?'; a red-hot ember is called a fire flower. Infinity is more than the hairs on a deer. . . . Old men are called mighty rocks; a hard-hearted person is 'he with a tree-trunk face'; when a person forgets what he is going to say he remarks that the bat carried off his story."

Thompson also noted that a careful choice of words can reduce unpleasantness. "If a tiger-ant bites you, say 'A dry leaf bit me,' for if you admit it was the bite of a tiger-ant, you will feel it for several days. A similar psychological routing of the odor of skunk is achieved by ignoring the skunk and remarking instead, 'How sweet is the scent of the squash seed my grandmother is toasting'. . . ."

Also in the spirit of their ancestors, the modern Maya feel most secure when they place themselves at the center of an organized universe. A cornfield in Yucatan has four sides, as did ancient earth, and is oriented in four sacred directions, with a fifth in the center. No matter what configuration a town has grown into, it is perceived as being square. In some isolated areas of the peninsula, citizens still mark a settlement's four sides with Christian crosses draped in embroidered fabric.

Highland municipalities also hold this comforting concept of homeland. People of the Guatemalan town of Quiche live in the center of a universe where sacred lakes and mountains of awesome power mark the four directions and the boundaries of their immediate world.

When a weaver of Chiapas pulls on a huipil and it settles evenly on her shoulders, she walks surrounded by woven designs that include statements of her lineage, the place where she lives, and saints and symbols that bring rain, fertility, and growth. Wherever she goes, then, she remains in the center of a mobile universe filled with harmony and renewal.

In their quest for equilibrium, the Maya cherish the deep spiritual bonds between generations, respect the role of humans in nature, and seek to balance their roles in the natural and supernatural worlds. "I see the Maya as almost Zen-like in their attitudes," says anthropologist James D. Nations of Conservation International in Washington, D.C. A young waiter in a hotel at the ruins of Uxmal recently described for me his way of life: "I have this work, and it pleases me. I have a little land, a rancho near here, with fruit trees, pigs, chickens. My wife and I have a new baby—that makes three children, and we don't plan any more. Life is complete. In some parts of Yucatan they are using a new word from English, 'stress.' But here there is tranquillity."

Most Maya remain traditional farmers, and respect for nature permeates their lives. Evon Z. Vogt of Harvard University lists five categories of sacred natural features in highland Chiapas: mountains, mountain passes, rocks, trees, and openings or depressions, such as caves and water holes. Most sacred are those that include a set of opposites—mountain and cave, up and down, revered ancestral god and dreaded Earth Lord. Vogt says that "such a geographic feature invariably has a 'cross' shrine which serves as a 'doorway,' a channel of communication to some deity in the cosmological system."

Mountains are thought to be the homes of benevolent highland ancestral gods—"fathers and mothers"—who preserve traditional ways and monitor activities of the living. In scattered municipalities such as Chamula and Zinacantan, traditionalists practicing a combination of Catholicism and ancient Maya religion light candles and offer prayers along with incense, food, and cane liquor at cross-marked shrines before ascending a mountain and again after reaching its peak. These rituals, writes Vogt, probably resemble "the behavior of the ancient Maya praying before stelae at the foot of pyramids and then climbing the steps to pray before idols in the temples on top. . . ."

In contrast to the ancestral gods, the highland Earth Lord, or earth owner, is a fat, cigar-smoking deity of mixed or of white blood. He lives underground, where he hoards enormous piles of money, large herds of cattle, horses, and mules, and flocks of chickens. Both fearsome and fascinating, he may, on whim, bless a person through generous gifts such as money or cattle. Vogt adds: "But this god, who needs many workers, may also capture a man and force him to work in the earth for years, until the iron sandals provided him wear out."

Like a dutiful ancient calendar god carrying a year through its course, men of Zinacantan and other highland municipalities assume the burden of an office and see their responsibility as their "cargo." This honor—this figurative burden and actual baton of authority—most often is gladly taken up by a cargo holder. Duties include administering civic legislation as well as overseeing religious festivals, usually with no small amount of personal financial obligation.

There are those, too, who still "keep the days" as the gods desired, counting the Maya calendar with grains of corn or seeds, and with the additional help of specially empowered stones, divining what the future holds in store.

But highland populations grow while the amount of arable land remains the same, and increasing numbers of Protestant Maya can add a factor of occasional local disharmony. New settlements of Protestants from Chamula ring the valley along the road that encircles the town of San Cristobal de las Casas. Early in 1992, a group of traditional Chamulans attacked them in their shantytowns.

Forty to fifty-five percent of Guatemala's 9,340,000 people are Maya. Guatemala's 30-year-long civil war has claimed 100,000 Maya dead and a million dispersed, and perhaps as many as 200,000 have fled to Mexico. "In June of 1993 about 45,000 Maya will be sent back to Guatemala," Jim Nations told me. "They will have been in Mexico ten years. Many of the children were born there but do not have citizenship, and the others have not lived in the highlands for decades. What will they go back to? Others settled on their land years ago."

In lowland Chiapas, where the Usumacinta and its tributaries flow, a farming people known as the Lacandon live. They have long been the most isolated—and the most traditional—of the lowland Maya. Jim Nations, who lived with them for several years and returns often, says there were some 300 Lacandon in 1980. "There are about 450 today. One of their villages, Naja, was once dispersed in the forest, and they lived traditionally; now they are clustering alongside an oil-exploration road, where the development is concentrated like a slum."

The Lacandon forest encompassed more than 5,000 square miles in 1943; today it measures some 2,120 square miles. The Mexican government began logging there as early as 1871, and timber production has accelerated. New non-Maya settlers clear land for cattle, and new roads have brought thousands more people.

"In the midst of this, in Naja, is Chan K'in, the old chief, who is about 90 now," says Jim. "Locals built a wall so he could have privacy in his thatched god-house, and there he is, doing a six-day-long ceremony to renew the power of the clay god-pots, while massive oil company trucks rumble past just outside. For ceremonies, the traditional Lacandon still make bark paper and dot it with red dye from annatto seeds; it looks like spots of blood. Usually it is the people 35 to 40 and older who are still conservative. The young are cutting their hair, wearing Western clothes, and driving trucks."

The fragile Lacandon forest is only the western extreme of the most extensive rain forest left on the North American continent. Like a vast jade canopy, it extends north through Quintana Roo and eastern Campeche in Mexico and south into Central America, covering much of Belize and Guatemala's Peten. From above, it seems an untouched wilderness, but the population of Peten alone has soared from 20,000 to more than 300,000 in the past three decades, as petroleum speculators, loggers, cattle ranchers, and landless peasants exploit this rich frontier. Some experts believe that, given the present rate of destruction, the forest will disappear by the year 2010. To protect their mutual forest, the governments of Guatemala, Mexico, and Belize have set aside ten million acres as reserves and national parks. The Maya, along with others living in buffer zones that edge protected areas, know that their future—as well as their past—lies within the forest.

Experts say that conservation combined with sustainable development is the solution. Anthropologist Mac Chapin of Cultural Survival, Inc., an indigenous-rights organization in Arlington, Virginia, points out that native peoples "have lived in the forests for centuries and have evolved production systems and ways of life that maintain the integrity of the natural environment." In Quintana Roo, cooperative farms are focusing on chicle production to keep the forest alive. Those living in buffer zones near the Maya Biosphere Reserve in northern Peten find that it is more profitable to harvest renewable resources like chicle, allspice, and ferns used by florists than to clear and destroy the forest for agricultural fields.

In addition to helping promote these projects, Conservation International encourages archaeological and ecological tourism. Of the tourists who travel to

Guatemala, 15 percent go to Peten's Tikal National Park to visit the ruins of the city and the rain forest that encircles it.

One new Maya enterprise, rooted in the past, sets its sights on survival and the future. On the north shore of Lake Peten Itza, a movement has developed in the town of San Jose, known as Motul de San Jose in the Colonial Period. But it is a far older settlement. Archaeologists found that in Classic times, pottery placed in a ruler's tomb at Dos Pilas had been presented by Motul's elite. Now a group of about 35 Maya at San Jose have taken a 50-year lease on 14 square miles of forest, which they call Bio Itza. Says Jim Nations, "They have only two requirements of those who join: You have to learn to speak Itza, and you can't cut down the forest. It's a 'back to the land' movement, a re-creation of Itza society."

Opposites, for the Maya, have always formed a whole, a completion. Today's contrasts of refugees and re-creation, of environmental destruction and preservation, of stress and tranquillity mark contemporary Maya lives just as they did those of their forebears.

A Maya friend in Merida—Guadalupe Cach, sister of my daughter-in-law Gloria—seems to epitomize a balanced and harmonious blend of modern and ancient. Frequently she packs a briefcase and jets off to Mexico City for a business meeting, but on Sundays she drives to the town of Ticul.

There she visits her large family, joins them in feasts of traditional foods, speaks Yucatec Mayan instead of Spanish, and admires the huipils her mother and sisters are embroidering. Family members joke and pun in Mayan. They speak of years spent living in the nearby ruins of Uxmal, where their father worked as a watchman. And they recall a great-grandfather who died long ago—they don't know the year—during a revolution, probably in the War of the Castes. But the young boys sit absorbed in a conflict they find more interesting—professional wrestling beamed from the States on cable television.

Ticul is an ancient town that is now a busy and prosperous center of pottery and shoe manufacturing. Yet no more than 200 miles to the south begins a vast and forbidding wilderness.

East of Piedras Negras, west of Tayasal, into northern Peten and southern Campeche, roads and settlements stop. Spread out maps and look closely; they show a few rivers and lakes. Some sites have been explored and a few studied, the huge cities of Calakmul and El Mirador among them. But there are enormous blank areas in this northern part of the rain forest. Indications of human impact seem hauntingly absent. Measure its miles by the hundreds: It is a mysterious, trackless land where few have ventured, filled with places no one knows. It is still the domain of the first creatures the old gods created, "all the guardians of the forest . . . the deer, birds, pumas, jaguars, serpents. . . ." It is likely a place of magnificent lost Maya kingdoms yet to be discovered.

Huddled in vivid contours, a Quiche Maya baby of Joyabaj, Guatemala, sleeps against its mother's back. In the highlands of Guatemala and Mexico, distinctive woven or embroidered designs indicate a person's native village.

Increasingly less traditional in dress, some men now wear Western clothes and hats. Most girls, however, embrace embroidery and weaving as a sacred duty, believing the saints—the first weavers—gave women the designs when the world began. Some rain and

fertility motifs still in use are so ancient—and meaningful—that they appear in art from more than a thousand years ago. Wrapped in a rainbow of shawl, a Quiche girl's shy smile lights a doorway in Nebaj.

GIANNI VECCHIATO (BOTH)

234

KENNETH GARRETT

236

*M*atrons find jovial companionship every day at the corn mill in Acanceh, Yucatan. Dried kernels that have been boiled and softened in a lime-and-water solution will be ground into dough by machine. Women once rose before dawn to spend hours grinding grain with stone manos and metates. Versatile masa—or corn dough—may be turned into any one of scores of traditional dishes, including tamales and tacos. More likely it will become tortillas, the staff of Maya life. Corn was the foundation of the Maya civilization, and the ancients revered it. Postclassic art depicts ritual food offerings— tamales made of turkey or iguana to delight the palates of the gods.

With everything balanced and harmonious—a Maya philosophical ideal—a family speeds along a highway near Oxkutzcab in Yucatan on the family bicycle, the most common form of private transportation on the peninsula. A ride of 15 or 20 miles and back while commuting to work, visiting friends and family, or marketing is not uncommon. Festive in the traditional embroidered huipil and white underskirt of Yucatan, the woman holds a machete, essential for cutting firewood and clearing thick bush, and a bulging basket of purchases. Truck farms and orchards in the fertile Puuc area make Oxkutzcab a garden spot of the peninsula. Large trucks—and humble bikes— crowd its cornucopian fruit and vegetable market.

DAVID ALLEN HARVEY

238

Wary Guatemalan guerrillas in a chance encounter along the Usumacinta River don masks and brandish M16 rifles before consenting to be photographed. Members of the Fuerzas Armadas Rebeldes (FAR), a Marxist group, these men participate in a civil war that has devastated Guatemala for 30 years. Often pitting Maya against Maya—as the rebels fight soldiers and military-controlled civilian guards—the war has destroyed many highland villages and left others inhabited almost entirely by women and children. Human-rights organizations estimate the conflict has claimed 100,000 lives, with 40,000 disappeared and a million dispersed—many to the sanctuary of refugee camps in Mexico. The conflict received worldwide coverage in October 1992, when a Quiche Maya woman, Rigoberta Menchú, long a critic of the Guatemalan military's human-rights abuses, was awarded the Nobel Peace Prize. The announcement called her "a vivid symbol of peace and reconciliation. . . ."

Innocence clad in the white of purity, a Maya girl kneels for absolution before taking her first communion in Telchaquillo, Yucatan. A bound Christ—in Spanish style—stands nearby. The girl has adopted the prevailing faith of the region, a harmonious blend of 16th-century Spanish Catholicism and ancient Maya beliefs.

FOLLOWING PAGES: Among the misty hills of the Puuc, farmer Santos Lopez tends his field. He harvests some ears and bends down the stalks of others to protect them from moisture as they dry. Attending to corn—a gift of the gods and the essence of the humans they created—is a duty his ancestors performed for the same reasons: for sustenance and for use in ancient rituals.

Acknowledgments

The Book Division is particularly grateful to Jeremy A. Sabloff, Professor of Anthropology at the University of Pittsburgh, who reviewed the text and illustrations in this book and provided expert advice and guidance during its preparation.

We would also like to thank the individuals named or quoted in the text and those cited here for their assistance: Robert M. Carmack, James A. DeYoung, George A. Lawrence, Jesus Eduardo Lopez Reyes, John McCullough, Walter F. Morris, Jr., and George E. Watson III.

Additional Reading

The reader may want to check the *National Geographic Index* for related materials; the Society has published many articles and books on archaeology in Mesoamerica. Earlier collaborations by Gene and George Stuart include *Discovering Man's Past in the Americas,* which contains much material on the Maya, as well as *The Mysterious Maya.*

The following were useful in the preparation of this book: Richard E. W. Adams, *Prehistoric Mesoamerica;* Elizabeth Benson, *The Maya World;* Robert M. Carmack, *The Quiché Mayas of Utatlán;* Michael D. Coe, *The Maya;* Elin C. Danien and Robert J. Sharer, eds., *New Theories on the Ancient Maya;* Bernal Díaz del Castillo, *The Discovery and Conquest of Mexico, 1517-1521;* William L. Fash, *Scribes, Warriors and Kings;* William M. Ferguson and Arthur H.

Rohn, *Mesoamerica's Ancient Cities;* Norman Hammond, *Ancient Maya Civilization;* John S. Henderson, *The World of the Ancient Maya;* Stephen D. Houston, *Reading the Past Maya Glyphs;* C. Bruce Hunter, *A Guide to Ancient Maya Ruins;* Joyce Kelly, *The Complete Visitor's Guide to Mesoamerican Ruins;* Mary Ellen Miller, *The Art of Mesoamerica;* Sylvanus G. Morley, George W. Brainerd, and Robert J. Sharer, *The Ancient Maya;* Walter F. Morris, Jr., *Living Maya;* Curt Muser, *Facts and Artifacts of Ancient Middle America.*

Also, A. R. Pagden, ed., *The Maya: Diego de Landa's Account of the Affairs of Yucatán;* Nelson Reed, *The Caste War of Yucatan;* Jeremy A. Sabloff, *The New Archaeology and the Ancient Maya;* Linda Schele and David Freidel, *A Forest of Kings;* Linda Schele and Mary Ellen Miller, *The Blood of Kings;* John Lloyd Stephens, *Incidents of Travel in Central America, Chiapas and Yucatan* and *Incidents of Travel in Yucatan;* Karl Andreas Taube, *The Major Gods of Ancient Yucatan;* Dennis Tedlock, translator, *Popol Vuh: The Mayan Book of the Dawn of Life;* J. Eric S. Thompson, *Maya History and Religion;* Alfred M. Tozzer, ed., *Landa's Relación de las Cosas de Yucatan;* Gianni Vecchiato, *Guatemala Rainbow;* and Evon Z. Vogt, *Tortillas for the Gods.*

Index

Boldface indicates illustrations.

Library of Congress CIP Data
Stuart, Gene S.
Lost kingdoms of the Maya / by
Gene S. Stuart and George E.
Stuart; prepared by the Book
Division of the National
Geographic Society.
p. cm.
Includes index.
ISBN 0-87044-928-1. --
ISBN 0-87044-929-X
(deluxe ed.)
1. Mayas. 2. Mayas--Antiquities.
3. Central America--Antiquities.
4. Mexico--Antiquities.
I. Stuart, George E. II. National
Geographic Society (U.S.). Book
Division. III. Title.
F1435.S88 1993   92-40803
972.81'016--dc20   CIP

Composition for this book by the Typographic section of National
Geographic Production Services, Pre-Press Division. Set in Palatino.
Printed and bound by R. R. Donnelley & Sons, Willard, Ohio.
Color separations by Graphic Art Service, Inc., Nashville, Tenn.;
Lanman Progressive Co., Washington, D.C.; Lincoln Graphics,
Inc., Cherry Hill, N.J.; and Phototype Color Graphics, Pennsauken,
N.J. Dust jacket printed by Miken Systems, Inc., Cheektowaga, N.Y.